H
LINC

HIDDEN
LINCOLNSHIRE

Adrian Gray

COUNTRYSIDE BOOKS
NEWBURY, BERKSHIRE

COUNTRYSIDE BOOKS
3 Catherine Road
Newbury, Berkshire

ISBN 1 85306 299 5

The front cover photograph of
Walesby church is reproduced by permission
of Lincolnshire County Council.

Produced through MRM Associates Ltd, Reading
Typeset by Paragon Typesetters, Queensferry, Clwyd
Printed by Woolnough Bookbinding, Irthlingborough

For Eleanor and Hannah

Introduction

▬ Lincolnshire is not quite as wild as it was when Henry VIII referred to it as the 'most brute and beastly shire' in his kingdom, but many parts of it are still surprisingly remote. There is, for example, not a mile of motorway in the present county, and this helps to keep hordes of traffic away, though there is a motorway through Humberside.

The county has many charms and in this book I have attempted to concentrate on two types of 'hidden' charm – forgotten buildings and forgotten stories about the places of Lincolnshire. Particular themes have emerged during my research – lost abbeys, 'holy' wells and secret underground passages. The disadvantage I have laboured under is that the county is so huge that it is impossible to include everything that I would wish; my apologies if I have omitted anyone's personal favourite. However, I am happy to hear of any suggestions for future editions of the book and also of any corrections that may need to be made; for things have a habit of appearing and disappearing.

Finally, please be aware that the mention of something in the text does not mean that there is automatic public access to it. One of the saddest aspects of modern Lincolnshire is the way in which much of its heritage is accidentally or deliberately made obscure. Too many houses are never open and one could mention the extraordinary Lincolnshire house that is hidden from view behind the sort of trees one would find on a 1970s housing estate . . . But there is much to enjoy.

Adrian Gray
Ruskington, June 1994

Aby and Belleau

➤ An enchanting area of many tiny settlements, Aby even has the shortest place name in Lincolnshire. As Aby was too small to look after a parish church this was demolished years ago, though the churchyard continued in use and was served by an iron mortuary chapel costing £95. The chapel, no longer in use, was dignified with the name of All Saints and was built on the site of the old church. For proper services, local people had to walk across to Belleau on the other side of the Great Eau.

Alford

➤ Alford, a delightful market town on the eastern fringes of the Wolds, seems to have had the most exciting period of its history in the 1600s. In 1630 the town was badly affected by the plague and virtually isolated for a while – rather like the more famous example of Eyam. Food for the people of Alford was left by kind villagers from neighbouring parishes at a stone cross on Miles Cross Hill, a mile outside the town on the Spilsby road.

The plague killed many that year. In a normal year there were about 19 deaths in Alford, but in 1630 the number rose to 131. One family lost six members in a week. The stone cross, where during the plague money had sometimes been left in vinegar so as not to be infectious, was moved in 1960 to the grounds of Tothby House near the town.

Like many Lincolnshire settlements, Alford had a Holy Well, which was still attracting 'pilgrims' into the 1830s.

There are a number of features of interest in the town. The church is unremarkable, but was said to have been badly damaged in a Civil War skirmish in June 1645. At the much more appealing manor house is an interesting folk museum, and Alford also has one of the best windmills in Lincolnshire.

A house in West Street once belonged to a builder who repaired churches. Collected fragments from these were used to decorate his garden.

Alkborough

◗ Almost the furthest corner of the historical county of Lincoln, the size of which can be understood if we consider that Alkborough is as near to Stamford as Stamford is to London. The village is dramatically positioned on the scarp slope of the limestone 'Cliff', overlooking the confluence of the Trent and the Ouse with the last yards of the former being marked by the Trent Falls.

These Falls are really deposits of sand and silt that become exposed at certain states of the tide, for the Trent is tidal for many miles south of here. It is believed that such deposits act as a barrier to the normal flow of the waters in a tidal river, restricting the inflow of the tidal current when this first starts to turn. The flow upriver is held back until sufficiently strong enough to mount the obstacles, and the normal downflow, being released in a sudden wave, runs upriver as the Aegir. This current is one of the natural phenomena of the region, but can be dangerous to the unwary river user.

The most famous feature of Alkborough itself is the turf maze known as Julian's Bower. The origins of this are very ancient and lost in mystery. As we might suspect, there are several versions to choose from. One school of thought maintains that the maze idea came from Troy and that Julian's Bower is named after Julius, the son of Aeneas. Another tradition links the maze idea to St Julian the Hospitaller, who killed his parents accidentally and, as a penance, set up a hostelry by a ford. One night when the 'hospital' was full, Julian gave his own bed to a wandering leper, who promptly turned into an angel. It has also been argued that the maze was constructed by the monks of a small monastic cell that existed here until the 13th century. This version maintains that the maze was used as a penance – sinners had to walk around it with hardened peas in their boots. Whatever its origins, to stand at Julian's Bower overlooking the Trent and the Humber is to enjoy one of the greatest scenes of Lincolnshire.

A copy of the maze is cut into the stone of the church porch, and this has been used over the years to recut the turf maze.

Julian's Bower – has a 44 foot diameter.

It is also present in the east window of the church and on the tomb of J. Goulton-Constable of Walcot, who was a great enthusiast for the maze.

Another feature of interest is the reredos in the church – the wooden screen behind the altar. This was produced in the 1920s by 'Mousey' Thompson, the Yorkshire wood-carver who began the tradition of including a carved mouse on furniture – in the case of church furnishings, very appropriate! At the back of the church, partially covered by a removable stone, is an old Roman pediment incorporated into a later arch, now at the bottom rather than at the top.

Just south of the Bower is Countess Close, an old camp whose name has been attributed to either the Countess of Warwick or to Countess Lucy, the wife of Ivo de Taillebois. Near here was also a Civil War battery, built in a wonderful position to command the entrance to the Trent.

Another story of Alkborough is that the church was rebuilt by the four knights who killed Thomas à Becket in Canterbury Cathedral. We can be fairly certain this is untrue, for if they cared so much for anonymity that they hid in Alkborough it is unlikely they would have all stayed together and built a church!

In the woods south of the village along the Cliff is a spring called the Kell Well. Any newcomer to the village who drank of its water was supposed never to move permanently from Alkborough. The vicinity was famous for its fossils, but the well is now almost inaccessible and much overgrown.

The Tower House, a tall brick house in the village, south of the maze, is unusual for having three storeys, but it is linked with a very sad tale. In about 1770 a small ship captained by a man named Wilkinson anchored offshore in the Humber to take on provisions. Wilkinson came into Alkborough, but while he was there a sudden squall blew up and struck his vessel, on board which was his wife and family. The poor man could do nothing but watch as the ship foundered and the family drowned. He determined to stay near to them until his own dying day, and reputedly built the tall house so he could watch over the spot where they died. Wilkinson died in 1809 and his gravestone can be found near the east wall of the church.

Alkborough's strategic position dragged it into the Civil War. The medieval cross in the churchyard was supposedly used by Parliamentarians in 1643 to sharpen swords, though it is also possible that the damage was done by men sharpening their arrows ready for a Sunday's archery practice. The Royalists are said to have barricaded themselves into the church.

Alvingham

➤ At Alvingham is a unique sight – two churches in one churchyard, both approached through the middle of a farmyard. The traditional explanation for this bizarre appearance is that in about 1150 some Gilbertine monks arrived to found a monastery in North Cockerington, south of the river Lud. Their building made good progress, but one morning they awoke to find that all their work had been shifted over the river to Alvingham and placed beside the church there!

The monks set to work demolishing the structure and carting everything back to their chosen site, but every night it was all returned to Alvingham. Eventually they gave up, and this is the reason for there being two churches in one churchyard. Another story relates that the churches were built by jealous sisters.

The true explanation is almost as complex. In fact they are the parish churches of Alvingham and North Cockerington and seem to share a common churchyard, though according to at least one description in the past, at that stage they were really in two different fields. The church of St Mary (now redundant) started life as the chapel to the Gilbertine priory, but eventually replaced North Cockerington's own church when that was demolished, although it was in Alvingham parish! However even this theory has been disputed, it being thought that St Mary's, North Cockerington was built by the lord of that manor in the 12th century. But why did he build it here? Behind the churches is a complex pattern of watercourses – the Louth Navigation, the old Lud and a drain to the watermill. To the west are the earthworks of the Gilbertine priory.

Close to the farmyard entrance is the other main feature of Alvingham, an attractive watermill that is sometimes open to the public. The present building dates from the 17th century and is fed by water that comes from the old river, under the canal, in a 60 yard tunnel. The recreated stocks in the village will also be noticed.

North Cockerington has a plague pit, a reminder that this area suffered as badly as other parts of the country from the Black Death and its related diseases.

Ancaster

➤ This is the town that controls the 'Ancaster Gap' through the limestone edge. It is believed that a major river once flowed through here, but the position brought an early interest from Iron Age tribes and from the Romans who established a major town on Ermine Street.

The Roman defences can be clearly seen close to the junction of the modern A153 with the B6403, which follows the Roman route. Various discoveries have been made over the years. Coins were found in Castle Close; in 1841 over 2,500 Roman coins – sold off to visitors as souvenirs. When a new cemetery was opened in 1909 it proved to have been accidentally sited on top on an ancient one. The village cross, which stands on the east side of Ermine Street, seems to have been made partially from a Roman milestone.

South of Ancaster, and accessible by public footpath, is 'the Valley', a delightful nature reserve of traditional meadow in a small valley probably cut by glacial waters. Its eastern edge borders what was a Roman road, branching off Ermine Street, to Bourne.

In the fields near **West Willoughby** is what appears to be an attractive but rather neglected house. In fact it is the stable block of Willoughby Hall, which was built in 1873 but later demolished.

Anwick

➤ Anwick seems almost a picture of certain aspects of Lincolnshire in miniature – a tiny fenside village, at the edge of which stands the functional buildings of a major agribusiness, the Padleys' chicken factory.

The secrets of the frozen chicken trade hardly come within the scope of this book, but the other secrets of Anwick certainly do. One of the most interesting of them is the Drake stones, which can be found at the south entrance to the churchyard.

The Drake stones are actually one large and one small chunk of Spilsby sandstone, brought to Anwick during the Ice Age and deposited there; as a textbook example of what geographers call a 'glacial erratic'. However, this is rather a dull explanation for a boulder or two being in the wrong place, so the Lincolnshire imagination has dressed up the story.

The stones are meant to have been found when a man was out ploughing with his horses in a field about half a mile to the north of the church. Horses and plough started to disappear into a sort of quicksand, the ploughman doing his utmost to rescue them but without success. Just as they finally disappeared into the bowels of the earth a 'drake' (or dragon) flew out from the ground. When villagers returned the next day, they found only a slight hollow and a stone shaped like a drake's head.

As the stone could not be moved, the Anwick villagers were unable to discover whether there really was treasure beneath it. Eventually it was ploughed under until enthusiastic local intellectuals, Dr Oliver and Rev Hazelwood, decided to rescue it. The stone was located and Dr Oliver attested that it was of druidic origin. Later, a traction engine was used to drag it to the church, where it seems to have broken into two.

Another version of how the stones got their name is less exciting – it is said that two drakes used to shelter there.

Anwick church contains a clock that was removed in 1927 from Tupholme Abbey, a nearby romantic ruin, and the village itself is notable for its round houses. The best of these is Anwick Forge, where two round houses dating from the 1790s have been joined by a central block to act as a tollkeeper's house and stopping place. The Sleaford to Tattershall Turnpike Trust was formed in 1793.

Anyone stopping in Anwick should also visit Parker's garden centre, which is tucked discreetly behind the church. This is the rural outpost of the famous bulb company.

Just to the north of Anwick, but a long way round by car as it lies on the minor road through Ruskington Fen, was the Anwick airfield which began life in 1916 during the campaign to stop Zeppelin attacks on Lincolnshire, but this did not

13

prevent bombs being dropped around the area in September 1917. A small plaque marks the spot. The airfield was revived in the Second World War as a 'decoy' field, but in March 1945 there was a serious accident between two Lancasters above the area and three men died.

Apley and Goltho

➤ Apley and Goltho are both so small that even together they hardly constitute a hamlet. In fact Goltho disappeared almost totally in medieval times, though subsequent excavation in 1974 has made it one of Lincolnshire's best known deserted medieval villages. South-west of the church were found the remains of many peasant houses and a manor house. Public footpaths cross the site.

Apley has fared little better. The church there fell down and so the current building actually started life as a mortuary chapel in 1871 – thus proving that there is life after death.

Just to the west is the parish of **Bullington**, similarly depopulated. At the edge of woodland off the Bullington to Stainfield road are earthworks, all that remains of Bullington Priory, which belonged to the Lincolnshire order of Gilbertines. Both monks and nuns lived there.

Appleby

➤ Appleby is the only village on the historic Ermine Street north of Lincoln, perhaps because the Romans chose to take their road away from the course of the limestone ridge where it bends to the north-west around modern Scunthorpe.

In the 1700s Appleby still had a 'Julian's Bower' (*see Alkborough*) near to the Roman road, but this had gone by the 1820s. There were also three old tumuli which featured as the village 'pinfold' (cattle enclosure). Any stray cattle were captured and their taking into custody was declared by a man with a bell on a Sunday. Any animal not redeemed after a year and a day was auctioned.

In about 1819 there was a strong feeling in the village about the conflicting merits of Anglicanism or Methodism. A passionate Methodist, Billy Braithwaite, liked to preach at the village cross but was told to go away by the estate steward, who had no real authority to do so. Braithwaite refused to leave the cross, so the steward got a crowbar from the smithy and with the help of two 'heavies', began to demolish it around the stubborn preacher. Braithwaite declared that if any of the three died a natural death then it would show they had been right and he had been wrong. The steward died in a fall off the church tower (symbolic, this!), one of the heavies managed to drown in a dyke that was only a few inches deep and the other was gored by a bull.

Appleby was a scene of the custom of 'riding the stee (or stang)'. If a man was known to beat his wife, the young people of the village would gather at the Stocks Tree to exact justice. For three nights they paraded the village with four people carrying a ladder (or 'stee') on which another sat. On the last night an effigy of the offending person was burnt outside his house and a mock funeral enacted.

Aswarby

➤ The A15 curves sharply around the park of the former Aswarby Hall, but the house itself was demolished in 1952, leaving the park as what has been unkindly called 'a moorish flat'. In fact it is an attractively open parkland, dotted with trees and including a real curio – what appears to be a tumulus surmounted with a tree, but may actually be the grave of a circus elephant which died near here in 1892. This is easily visible from the main road, just north of the Tally-Ho Inn.

The house here has had a long history. It was one of the properties that were snapped up by the rapidly rising Carre family in the 1500s, but one of their descendants was insane and this led to unseemly battles for control in the mid-1600s. One of the Carres was rumoured to have been the father of Horace Walpole, but it was never proved. Curiously, in the 1730s Aswarby was one of the Lincolnshire settlements to enjoy a brief fame as a spa because of its springs.

In the church is a memorial to George Bass, the explorer,

born here in 1771. He joined the Navy as a surgeon and helped the explorer Matthew Flinders to chart the coast of Australia. Bass disappeared on a voyage in 1803, and was assumed to have been killed and eaten by a Maori named Honekai who 'has never been well since he killed the man'.

Bardney

◥ There are a few scant remains of Bardney Abbey to be seen, all that is left in situ of one of the most important of the county's monasteries. It predates the Norman Conquest by three centuries but was refounded in about 1087 having been devastated by Danish invaders.

Bardney Abbey is especially associated with the tale of St Oswald, who was killed in AD 642. In addition to being impaled, his head, hands and arms were cut off. Years later his body was brought to Bardney by his niece but was refused entry by the monks. A miracle was necessary to convince them of the foolishness of their ways, a pillar of light appearing in the night sky. To protect them from Danish attacks, in about AD 910 Oswald's remains were taken to Gloucester.

A result of this event was the tradition that Bardney people should never close their doors in case similar events happen again. It must have made Bardney a popular place with robbers.

Bardney church was once at the abbey, but a new one was built in the 15th century, apparently after a campaign by villagers, including the disruption of the monks' services. Inside the church are various fragments from the abbey. An altar stone dug up in 1873 was assumed to be St Oswald's stone from the abbey.

Bardney airfield was a bomber station in the Second World War. In 1943 it contributed to an attack on the *Tirpitz* and in 1945 George Thompson won the VC by beating out the flames on his aircraft with his hands; he died of burns three weeks later.

Barlings

➤ The Abbey of Barlings can be found at the end of a quiet lane, beside the Barlings Eau on the edge of the fenland. The Premonstratensian abbey was founded in 1154 on the slightly raised ground of Oxeney (Ox Island) close to the Eau, which was navigable for at least some of the time that the abbey was there. Grange Farm may mark the first site used by the monks, before they moved closer to the river. The monks built large fishponds on the site, which are readily recognisable, though only a small piece of actual building remains as the tower fell down in 1757.

In 1267 the Abbey of Barlings was bequeathed some money so that it could build and maintain a chantry chapel at Langworth, a settlement which has now overtaken Barlings in importance. It has been suggested that Langworth was actually a 'planned town', set up by the monks to gain extra revenue, perhaps from travellers along the old Roman road. The church there now is interesting, but not because of any connection with the monks. In fact it is the reconstructed chapel of Walmsgate Hall, pieced back together in 1960-2 after being brought from the eastern Wolds.

Barlings was active in the 1536 revolt against Henry VIII's religious policies. The abbot actually took some of his canons to meet the rebels at Horncastle – dressed in full armour. The abbot later paid for this decision by being executed at Tyburn.

Barnetby-le-Wold and environs

➤ Barnetby-le-Wold is a classic example of a village whose morphology has been dramatically changed by the introduction of the railway. The old church of Barnetby sits halfway up the scarp slope of the Wolds, but the village has grown in the opposite direction towards the station. The church stands close to springs and a 'holy well' once renowned for restoring eyesight.

The area is well known for the Melton Gallows, which can be seen on the A18 just west of the turning for Barnetby-le-

Wold. It is said the gallows was put up on the orders of James I as the result of a feud between the Tyrwhitt and Ross (or Roos) families; the former family was from Kettleby. One day they met while out hunting and there was a fight which resulted in the deaths of several of their retainers. The king decided to erect the gallows as a warning to his subjects to maintain more orderly relations.

In fact the feud between the two families predates the gallows by about 200 years. Because of a land dispute in 1411 Sir Robert Tyrwhitt and 500 men laid waste William de Roos' manor of Melton Ross, following which the Roos family complained to the king and the archbishop. Tyrwhitt had to confess his fault and provide a banquet for all the men involved at his own expense. Strangely, Tyrwhitt was a justice of the court of King's Bench.

According to another tradition, the gallows did claim a victim. Some schoolboys were once playing there and decided to play at hanging. Just as a three-legged hare ran by, one of them slipped and actually did hang himself, the others running away in terror. The hare is believed to be a symbol of a witch. The gallows there today is obviously a re-creation, and seems rather too short to hang any adult. But perhaps this is deliberate, lest there should be any hares about.

Between Melton Hall and the railway are extensive remains of the medieval moated site of Melton manor and its fishponds.

The Tyrwhitt house at **Kettleby** was demolished in 1697, the house there now having been built in 1768 but sited amidst the earthworks and moats of the old one. It was the Tyrwhitt home from the 14th century and here Henry VIII stayed in 1541. When the nearby railway was being built it ran through the ancient burial ground and many old coffins were disturbed. A local Catholic priest showed some interest in them, so the navvies decided that they must be Catholic coffins and treated them with disrespect; the bodies were later reburied at **Bigby**. There was a medieval village at **Kettleby Thorpe** but is has been ploughed over.

There are some related tombs in Bigby church, including one of a later Sir Robert Tyrwhitt, who died in 1581. His tomb includes a portrayal of the common Lincolnshire feature, a hairy 'wild man'.

Barely half a mile to the south is the shrunken hamlet of **Somerby**. The monument nearby was put up by Edward Weston in 1770 to commemorate 29 years of happy marriage.

The next hamlet to the south, along the spring line, is **Searby**. The vicar here for 44 years of the Victorian era was Rev T. Townshend, who loved carving wood. He has left various features in the church interior, such as the screen and the pulpit, and a delightful shelter outside. This was intended for the coachmen and horses to use during services and was inscribed 'Rest and be thankful'.

Searby, Somerby and other villages in the area were largely depopulated due to Richard Rossiter, the lord of Somerby in the early 1600s. He enclosed his previously arable land so that he could introduce stock-farming, thus requiring fewer farm labourers. He was then able to justify demolishing much of his parish church as it was no longer needed!

Barnoldby-le-Beck

A small and prosperous village that is really part of Grimsby suburbia. It had been a fief of the Pelhams of Brocklesby – there is a house called Pelham House that was supposedly once a hunting lodge.

In a narrow lane to the north-east of the church is an unusual memorial. This is to William Smith, a huntsman, who fell from his horse and was killed in April 1845, though the obelisk was not put up until 1862. Smith was one of several generations of Smiths who acted as hunt servants for the Pelhams of Brocklesby.

The manor house at Barnoldby is not of great interest, but it is unusual in having had someone buried in its garden. Susannah Hewson died in the 17th century but for religious reasons had declared herself opposed to burial in the churchyard, so she was buried in her garden.

Barrow-upon-Humber

► A settlement of ancient importance, but now not much more than a village. It is believed that this is where St Chad founded an abbey called Ad Baruae in the 7th century, and that he was buried here. The north end of the village is known as St Chad and the remains of a Saxon church have been found there.

At **Barrow Haven** there was once a substantial Norman castle. Its earthworks look impressive in the flat marshland, but its principal defences would have been water. It may have been built by the Count of Aumale to protect his ferry across the Humber. This remained an important ferry crossing for many years – Henry VIII used this route on his progress through the county in 1541.

The discoverer of longitude, John Harrison, moved to Barrow in 1697. In 1731, his brother James made the sundial in the churchyard reusing part of the medieval cross. Together they designed, and in 1735 produced, a clock that would keep time at sea and enable longitude to be calculated.

Although Barrow gradually lost its ferry to Barton, from 1825 a new ferry service began from Oxmarsh near Barrow. This may have originated in a smuggling operation, for the name of New Holland has often been linked with Holland's gin. The new ferry station won the contract for handling the Hull mails in 1836 and soon had railway connections as well. It was a fascinating place until the opening of the Humber Bridge in 1980 killed off the coal-fired paddle steamers.

Barton-on-Humber

► Barton is one of the most important towns in the north of Lincolnshire; up to 200 years ago it was more important than Grimsby; and Scunthorpe, of course, is a comparative *nouveau riche* among towns.

The first surprising thing about Barton is that it has two churches, barely 300 hundred yards apart, and separated by a blow well that does not always contain water. The well, once considerable in size and filling the grassed area between the churches, is reputed to be the site where St Chad baptised many of the early Christians of Lindsey in the 7th century. As such it is a fascinating site of great spiritual significance to the county, as is the church of St Peter to the east of it. There have been other important wells in the town, for example at the junction of Fleetgate and Burgate, where there was also a chapel, again indicative of some spiritual significance.

Barton was important in Saxon times when it was enclosed within substantial defences. The footpath running south-east from St Paul's graveyard actually follows part of the course of the defences, though the town centre has now migrated westwards. The Saxons built a substantial church here, which is one of the ancient treasures of Lincolnshire, now in the care of English Heritage. The tower here is one of the most striking features, but equally interesting is the baptistry on its west side – showing that Chad's Pool was soon replaced by more comfortable conditions.

Yet there is another church close by – and a bigger one. The traditional explanation of this is that St Paul's was in the control of the monks of Bardney Abbey and, resenting this, the townspeople built their own church of St Mary.

Like several other places in the county, Barton has a curfew bell legend. It is related that an old lady got lost in the fields around Barton but was guided to safety by the sound of the church bells. She gave some land, from which the revenues were to be used to ring the bells for an hour at dusk from the harvest of the first barley until Shrove Tuesday. The traditional name was therefore the 'Barley Bell', which seems to have stopped ringing in about 1860.

In Fleetgate was once the Ferry Boat Inn. Its position showed how the shore of the Humber had retreated, but it was also associated with an interesting legend. In 1745 there was much fear of an invasion by Bonnie Prince Charlie. When three rough-looking strangers in Highland dress were seen in Barton it was assumed that they were the advance guard of a huge force, so everyone barricaded their homes. The constable refused to help, claiming that he had no warrant for their arrest, and went to bed. The Scots saw that the door of the

Ferry Boat was still open, so two of them went inside and helped themselves to food, making sure that the landlady had seen their sharp swords.

The landlady fled for help to the miller. He attacked the men by throwing bags of flour into their faces, disabling them long enough to have them pinned down. They were locked up for the night in a chantry chapel but escaped through a hole in the roof and fled. There was a rumour that the miller's wife helped them to escape as she did not wish to see them hanged.

There are two important houses in Barton. One of these is Baysgarth House, now a very interesting museum. Close to St Peter's is Tyrwhitt Hall, dating back to medieval times, and effectively the manor of Barton. On the Humber marshes can be found the Far Ings nature reserve which makes effective use of old clay pits.

Barton is one of several places in the county that are associated with whale bones. A beached whale is supposed to have been the origin of some rib bones (once believed to be jaw bones) that were used to decorate Westfield Road.

Bassingham

Outside the east window of Bassingham church is the grave of Arundell Leakey, a former clergyman of the parish. He is probably the only man from Bassingham to have had two funerals!

Leakey had been the incumbent at Bassingham for a number of years when he developed a depressive brain disease. In July 1924 he shot himself in the head while in bed, and the coroner recorded a verdict of suicide during a fit of temporary insanity. His funeral at Bassingham was taken by the rural dean who omitted the words 'sure and certain hope of resurrection' over the graveside, taking the view that Leakey's suicide was a mortal sin.

This behaviour outraged the Rev Roome, Leakey's London clergyman friend, and his colleague from the neighbouring village of Aubourn. Roome called the first funeral service a 'parody' that had 'wantonly outraged' the whole village. So the two men conducted another funeral the next day, saying all the correct words at the graveside, although the body was already buried.

The street name Torgate is derived from the local word for flax – 'tor' or 'taw'. Flax was much grown around here in the 18th century but declined sharply in the 19th.

Belton (Isle of Axholme)

➤ Here is a good example of the Lincolnshire problem of place names occurring twice or even more often within one county!

In medieval times the district, now part of Humberside, would have been best known for Temple Belwood, a 'hospital' of the Knights Templar, but now has little to see – and a motorway passing more or less through the middle.

However, in the church can be found the tomb of Richard of Belwood, a medieval knight. Apparently this was opened in the 16th century and the knight's bones uncovered. He was found to be wearing a pair of slippers.

There was much trouble here during the draining of the carrs. At Sandtoft the church was defaced by local people and carrion was apparently buried beneath the altar in protest. The house of Nathaniel Reading, one of the leading forces in the drainage scheme, was demolished by an angry crowd so he built a new one in Belton in 1697. They set that on fire and tried to block the keyholes so he could not escape. However he died in Belton in 1716 at the age of 100.

In the 19th century Belton got a new rector – a man who had come into a fortune of £30,000. He spent his money freely and it was said that the church was always full, though one must doubt the motives of at least some of the congregation. Money was lavished on a new cottage for the gardener, land for the needy, and on the church building. Soon it was all gone and the congregation dwindled away – there were even accusations that the rector was a swindler.

Definitely worth a visit, rather than a glance whilst passing on the motorway, is the obelisk close to the lane that runs out of Belton to Beltoft. This is a genuine folly, for it was erected by a grief-stricken squire in memory of his favourite hunting

The obelisk at Temple Belwood — memorial to a horse?

mare. There is a rumour that the squire vowed to give up hunting after the death of his beloved steed, so he shot his two best dogs and buried them either side of the mare!

Bicker

An attractive although rather straggling village that was once a port. It owes its meandering shape to the way it is strung out along a watercourse even today. The estuary of Bicker Haven, which gave it its importance, reached as far as the Red Lion public house near the main road. This accounts for the large and impressive church, set delightfully in tree lined lanes with a stream flowing between deep banks.

The remains of an old stone cross in the church once had pieces of chain attached at the foot. It was said that these were used to retain a horse, or occasionally a criminal if the lock-up was full.

On the path between the old rectory and the church is a row of graves for various members of the Holmes family. One of these is to Hezekiah Holmes and is inscribed:

'Underneath this solitary sod
There lies a Man
Whose ways was very odd
What ever his faults where [sic]
Let them alone
Let thy utmost care be
To mend thy own.
Let him that free from sin
First cast a stone.'

In 1941 fourteen high explosive bombs were dropped on Bicker, but none exploded. A tablet of thanks in the church commemorates this event.

Billingborough

Not one of the most attractive 'towns' of the area, but the surrounds of the church are notable for the wells that can be found there. The name of Billingborough was once assumed to be derived from 'Boiling borough', but is more likely to be derived from the name of a family or tribe – hence Billinghay, a few miles north.

Of the springs, it is notable that by reputation one was said to be a chalybeate spring though that next to it was not, yet they are very close. The wells are said to have failed only twice ever, and to have healing properties.

Billingborough Hall is also said to be built with stone from Sempringham Priory.

Binbrook

Binbrook is a decayed market town that has suffered from being in an area of declining population between its larger rivals Market Rasen and Louth. In 1749 a bad fire destroyed many of the houses, from which the town never really recovered. A visitor in 1780 described it:

'It is only remarkable for the number of fine eels caught in the river. The town consists of one street which is so dirty as to be little better than a common road, and the houses are mean buildings.'

Once it was large enough to support two churches – St Mary's and St Gabriel's, but now it just has one church dedicated to both saints. The 'lost' church of St Gabriel was on the north side of the Market Place and a few signs of its churchyard remain. It collapsed in 1822 and was left in ruins for many years. St Mary's was demolished in 1867 and replaced by a design of the Louth architect, James Fowler.

There is a large airfield to the north-west, opened in 1940. During the war against Hitler the airfield was 'defended' by an arrangement of wooden poles and hay-stuffed figures supposed to look like anti-aircraft guns and their crews.

Two miles west is the hamlet of **Stainton-le-Vale**. This was one of the last outposts of a common Lincolnshire tradition of 'mumping'. Each St Thomas's Day (21st December) one member of a family was allowed to go around the houses of farmers and other well-to-do residents, collecting wheat to make frumenty by mixing it with raisins and sugar.

Kirmond-le-Mire is another remote Wolds hamlet. However, it was a well-known area to the Romans, who had a large villa to the north of the church near the old village of Beckfield.

Biscathorpe

━ Biscathorpe is a remote Wolds hamlet and an excellent example of a 'lost' village. Its extensive earthworks can be seen to the north of the church. To the south, a footpath follows the river Bain to a small lake. These waters feed down to the mill at **Donington-on-Bain**, where the ghost of a murdered woman is said to glide across the waters.

North of Biscathorpe is Grim's Mound, a burial mound in the past associated erroneously with the Grim legend, which itself is linked to the founding of Grimsby. Here we also have the hamlet of **Grimblethorpe**. There are other barrows along High Street to the west of Burgh ('Bruff').

This is one of the main concentrations of deserted villages. Apart from Biscathorpe itself, there are **East and West Wykeham, Calcethorpe** and **South Cadeby** within a mile or two of each other. East Wykeham has the remains of its church.

Blankney

━ Blankney is the estate village par excellence, except that the hall is now a ruin, never rebuilt after a fire in 1945, and much of the park has become a golf course. The hall is supposed to have been burnt down when someone left an iron on! However, one can gaze through the gates of the hall and look upon its sad remains, visualising how things must once have been . . .

The hall is most commonly linked with the Chaplin family but the first of these was not at Blankney until 1719 when Thomas Chaplin bought the estate. Its previous owner, Lord Widdrington, had been found guilty of treason in the 1715 rebellion and there was a persistent rumour that he had hidden his treasure in a vault beneath the stairs. During the 19th century this vault was uncovered and a great chest found inside. Imagine the disappointment when it was opened and found to contain only a salt cellar and an iron ladle.

Henry Chaplin was an MP from 1868 to 1906 and his era

was the heyday of Blankney which was even visited by the Prince of Wales. However Chaplin was unlucky in love, for he was jilted by Lady Flora Paget who married the Marquis of Hastings instead. The two men continued to be rivals on the race-track, culminating in the victory of Chaplin's horse Hermit in the 1867 Derby, which was expected to be won by Hastings' Vaubon. Hastings lost £120,000 betting on his own horse and was ruined.

Someone else who bet on this race was Sir John Astley of Elsham Hall. He put a bet on a horse at 20-1 and could have gone off with £8,000 had it not been for Hermit. However he did see his own choice before the race and found that it had 'a languid air as if he was more likely to die on the course than win the great race.' Astley reported that Chaplin himself won nearly £100,000 and when he heard of Astley's misfortune paid his losses for him with good grace – though Astley made sure he paid it back later!

The Chaplins ensured that life in Blankney was according to their wishes. Thus the village had no pub or Nonconformist chapel, but they did have a club and a library and these can still be seen.

Boothby Pagnell

➤ 'The most important small Norman manor house in England', according to *The Buildings of England*, is tucked away in Lincolnshire just a few miles off the A1. All but invisible to the passing traveller is this ancient building that one would have thought should have generated a few road signs, a proper historical display and possibly enough trade to support a tea-shop or two.

Boothby Pagnell manor house is hidden away behind the hall, like a garden shed that rather outgrew its status. Dating from around 1200 it was once fortified by a moat and makes an interesting contrast to the houses of a similar date on Steep Hill in Lincoln.

It is possible to see the house, if you do not have an appointment, by following a footpath around the west side of the hall grounds. From this path can be seen another curio of Boothby Pagnell – a Norman church font which has been turned into the head of a well.

A famous rector of Boothby Pagnell from 1619 to 1660 was Dr Robert Sanderson, who also became Bishop of Lincoln. A man of strong beliefs, he abandoned what could have been a glittering academic career at university to do parish work.

During the Civil War he became enmeshed in religious politics. Finding it impossible to avoid trouble, he was once taken hostage to secure the release of the rector of Allington, whose views were markedly different, and in 1648 was arrested – he is also rumoured to have been shot at while preaching in his own pulpit.

The Norman manor house

Boston

➤ The most famous feature of Boston is, of course, the Stump, which can hardly be included in a book on 'Hidden' Lincolnshire as it is visible for miles around. However, one of the secrets of the Stump is its odd links with the calendar—there are said to be 60 steps to the rood loft, 24 to the library, 7 doors, 52 windows, 12 pillars and 365 steps to the top of the tower.

A less well-known corner of Boston is Pump Square, which used to be one of the town's main sources of water. Under the Square were two stone vaults which filled with water, and could then be pumped out. Close by is the Freemasons' Hall, possibly the only neo-Egyptian building in Boston (or even Lincolnshire). Just why the Boston freemasons decided that Egyptian architecture suited their pretensions is as mysterious as the order's own rituals.

Also something of a mystery is the Hussey Tower, which is missed by most visitors to Boston as it sits on the edge of the main town in an unattractive area. Built in the mid-1400s, it was probably part of a larger house that was being dismantled little more than a century after it was built. It belonged to the Hussey family of whom Lord John Hussey was the least favoured, being executed at Lincoln for failing to do anything except run away during the Lincolnshire Rising of 1536. He had 'a shifty look and beady eyes' according to Sir Francis Hill, the Lincoln historian, and after his death much of his property was confiscated, including Hussey Tower.

Fishtoft parish covers much of eastern Boston including the Pilgrim Hospital, but the actual village is about two miles to the south-east. It was once famous for the hawthorn tree that was a noted sight at the junction of the roads to Freiston and to Rochford Tower, close to Fishtoft church. A legend recorded that this was where a female suicide had been buried, and a stake of hawthorn had been been driven into her body to prevent her return as the 'undead'. However, it was the stake that came back to life, growing into a tree.

The parish church is dedicated to Guthlac, the famous Crowland saint. A statue of him has stood on the west face of the tower for many years, though he has lost an arm in the past. Guthlac is usually depicted carrying a whip, and it was Fishtoft tradition that as long as he held a whip there would be no mice or rats in the parish.

The other sight in Fishtoft is the Rochford Tower, one of a series of tower-houses built in Lincolnshire during the 1400s. It is similar to the Hussey Tower in Boston.

Bourne

Though in the past its history has been considerably embroidered, Bourne has some interesting features that make it one of the county's best market towns.

Firstly, as its name suggests, the town would not exist without water. There is an important spring at Peter's Pool where the wellhead could be relied upon for centuries until modern extraction techniques began to threaten it. Out of the town is 'Blind Well', close to Bourne Wood, one of a number of chalybeate springs in the county linked with the cure of eyesight problems.

Close to the wellhead is the site of Bourne castle, which was important for many centuries. The castle is said to have been destroyed by the Danes in AD 870 after the battle at Threekingham, but was more popularly associated with Hereward the Wake who supposedly launched his frenzied attack on the Normans here. Attractive as it would be to think that Hereward placed Norman heads on poles in the middle of Bourne, there is no real proof of the story.

Bourne remained an important town in Norman times and also gained from an abbey being founded in the 12th century. The parish church is a survival of this. Bourne's most famous monk was Robert Mannyng in about 1300, who wrote *Handlyng Synne* and *Chronicle of England* in English – very unusual at a time when Latin was the accepted written language. He was probably a native of Bourne and was a monk at Sempringham and Sixhills, though the full details of his life are not known.

More fanciful stories are attached to Red Hall. This was built in the early 17th century; it has been claimed as the scene of

Sir Everard Digby's machinations in the Gunpowder Plot. This is probably because the house once belonged to a leading Catholic, Sir John Thimbleby. In the 19th century it was used by the railway company as a booking office and ladies' waiting room before proper accommodation was provided on the nearby platforms. Since then the Red Hall has been rather better cared for.

Quiet though it is, Bourne was once the centre of the British motor-racing industry. This was because Raymond Mays, the founder of the BRM team, was born and lived at Eastgate House. By 1939 he had become the leading British racing driver and after the war set up BRM to build racing cars in the old maltings behind his house in Bourne; he also bought the old gasworks yard next door. The cars were tested at Folkingham airfield, but in 1959 the Air Ministry stopped this arrangement when Folkingham was used to test rockets.

In Bourne cemetery is the old pump from the Market Place.

Brant Broughton

Brant Broughton has two exceptionally interesting religious buildings.

The parish church is beautiful on the outside, with a soaring spire and some impressive gargoyles. Inside, it is even better. The fascination of Brant Broughton church is that the interior is exceptional because of one man – Canon Sutton, the rector from 1873 to 1888, who believed that the creation of beautiful things was an important way of worshipping God. A perfectionist, he had the stained glass windows fired in a kiln at the rectory and much of the ironwork – such as the candelabra which grace the chancel – made at the village forge by blacksmith Fred Coldron. The result is richly satisfying. While there, pause outside at the east end of the church to note the steps made from old gravestones.

In the 17th century Brant Broughton had a history of religious turbulence. During the later years of the century, Thomas Robinson disturbed church services by accusing the rector of being a false prophet who took his stipend but did nothing to justify it. Robinson incurred many legal problems

A medieval carved head on the church doorway.

because of his attitude to the Anglican church, but the authorities were notably reluctant to make him suffer, even though the Nottinghamshire authorities requested that he be fined for preaching in their territory.

Eventually Robinson became a Quaker, and the Quaker Meeting House was converted from a barn in 1701. It can be visited in Meeting House Lane.

Bratoft and Gunby

These two hamlets are linked together due to their association with the Massingberd family and Gunby Hall.

The original home of this family was at Bratoft, where their house was demolished in 1698 when they moved to Gunby.

The moated site of their original home is well worth a visit, and is accessible by public footpath a few hundred yards north of the church. Part of a brick bridge is the most substantial remnant.

Bratoft church is notable mainly for the unusual allegorical painting of the Spanish Armada, with the Armada being characterised in paint and poetry as a dragon.

The estimated date for the construction of Gunby Hall fits very neatly with the demolition of the Bratoft house. But the former is so well known through its links with the National Trust that it will not be dealt with in detail here.

Brattleby

Brattleby is a small cliff-edge village just north of Scampton airfield. The sound of modern jets is rather incongruous in an ancient settlement; the church dates back to the 11th century and is said to have been marked by Danish fires.

The parish stretches up onto the top of the limestone, where huge flocks of geese were once reared on the Heath. Here, too, is a small wood reputed to have been the scene of a battle between the forces of King Stephen and Matilda. There is said to be the ghost of a white lady, who rides around on a horse looking for her dead lover.

Brigg

Brigg, now in Humberside, is an attractive town well worth a visit, however it was originally just a hamlet of Wrawby, its spiritual needs being served by a hermit in an oratory. Although the motorway passes it by, Brigg has featured in human activity for a long time. Near to the present river crossing have been found the remains of a Bronze Age planked causeway and two ancient boats. The causeway was discovered at the northern end of Island Carr in 1884, and on the east bank of the Ancholme two years later the first of the boats, nearly 50 ft long and hollowed out of a tree. This boat was exhibited in Hull and was an unfortunate victim of Nazi air-raids in 1943. In 1888 another boat was discovered to the north of the causeway site, contributing to a four year period which made Brigg archaeologically famous.

Brigg is now a small but bustling market town with Wrawby Street well on the way to being given 'heritage' treatment. But the town has built its success on a curious mixture of activities – at one time it exported rabbit pelts from the Normanby and Roxby warrens and in 1654 was said to be famous for 'plantations of licorice'.

One of the most famous sights in the town is in Bigby Street, where the Dying Gladiator pub is adorned with a lifelike dying gladiator. At times in the past he has been realistically, even gorily, painted, but on a recent visit he looked badly in need of reviving. The Angel is also a notable inn.

Brocklesby

Brocklesby is the premier aristocratic estate in northern Lincolnshire and, with apologies to Belton, probably in the whole county. So influential has it and the Pelham family been, that when the boundary between Lincolnshire and Humberside was drawn in 1974 it followed a contorted route to ensure that Brocklesby continued to be part of Lincolnshire.

We can hardly call the house at Brocklesby 'hidden' but many interesting features of the estate are less well known and thus worthy of mention here. The grounds were laid out by 'Capability' Brown in 1771 and include many items of interest that pre and post-date his work. For example, south of the church there is the Holgate Monument with its curious design of an urn supported by three tortoises. This is a monument to an apparently rather subservient tenant of the Yarboroughs, and nearby can also be found memorials to a dog and a horse.

In Mausoleum Woods to the south are several other curiosities. There is the Mary Carter Temple, dating from the 1700s and a grotto dating from the height of Gothic melodrama in the early 1800s. Near to that is the Hermitage, really a form of root house where, of course, a hermit is supposed to have lived. The fourth item in this group is the temple of Arabella Aufrere, again late 1700s.

Architecturally, the most important building in the Brocklesby area is the mausoleum on the edge of **Great Limber** said to be on a tumulus. This widely regarded as the masterpiece of James Wyatt and is a stunningly beautiful building, both inside and out. It is also irresistible as it is so tragically romantic – a grieving memorial to a young wife who died at the age of 33 in 1786. The grief-stricken mood is most evident inside the building, with its subdued light and the figure of Sophia Aufrere. Here is one of the highlights of Lincolnshire.

East of Great Limber are the remains of a Cistercian priory, c1376, said to have had only two monks.

West of Brocklesby on the B1210 can be found the Memorial Arch, built in 1864-5 in memory of the 2nd Lord Yarborough.

Just north of the B1211 towards Ulceby was Newsham Abbey, a monastery founded in 1143 of which little remains. Near to it Capability Brown built the rather unusual Newsham Bridge, with its seven arches.

Burgh-le-Marsh

➤ An attractive market town that comes as a delightful surprise after the drab exit on the main road out of Skegness. The town was once important enough to have had two churches, but St Mary's was destroyed in the 1500s and its site taken over by Baptists; the churchyard later became a garden.

The church is one of a number in the county with a story attached to its bell-ropes. According to the legend, a ship was in trouble off the coast (then closer than it is now). The captain heard the sound of Burgh's bells and was able to guide his vessel away from dangerous waters. Captain Frohock was so grateful that he gave an acre of land at Orby to be used to pay for replacement silk bell-ropes at regular intervals.

Cock Hill, a large mound in the middle of the town, gets its name from its use in the 1700s for cock-fighting. Roman and Anglo-Saxon material has been found close by, but stories about it being a prehistoric burial site are untrue.

Burgh-le-Marsh lost its railway station in 1970, but the station house has been put to good use serving teas, and the old goods yard is the home for a small railway museum, where the exhibits include a narrow-gauge railway. There is also a windmill on the eastern edge of the town that is worth visiting.

Burton upon Stather

Burton is almost two separate villages, for there is Burton upon Stather on the Cliff and **Burton Stather** by the river Trent. The word 'Stather' derives from staiths, meaning wharf. The view from the churchyard at the former is almost dramatic and has been described as being one of the finest in Lincolnshire; it was once regarded as a beauty spot for Gainsborough folk to visit by steamer.

Burton has had a rather chequered history. It was once a market town but this function had almost died out by the 1600s (a plaque on the church wall guides you to the market place location), perhaps partly due to a 'tempest' which was said to have destroyed many of the houses. In 1643 the Civil War came to Burton and is remembered in the name of Barracks Yard, inspired by the use of it by the Royalists, who were ousted from their stronghold by Parliamentary forces from Hull in December 1643. A book written in 1769 claimed that Burton once had two churches, one of which nestled so close under the Cliff that it was almost possible to jump onto its steeple.

In 1770 the area suffered from bad flooding and in 1777 much of the village was badly damaged when a shipload of gunpowder blew up a mile away. Though no one was killed at Burton, the cost of repairs was a very considerable £3,000.

The springs along the Cliff have been known to produce 'petrified' mussels, cockles and 'snake stones'. Foremost among these springs was St Aniel's Well, which was at the foot of the hill in Burton Wood. It was said to be excellent for curing old wounds and sores, though the several local people I spoke to had never heard of it! However there is a good example of a spring by the picnic site on the road to Alkborough.

To the east at **Thealby** is a Quaker burial ground. It is also worth visiting Normanby Hall, less than a mile from Burton. This attractive country house is now maintained by Scunthorpe Borough Council. Of particular interest is the old ice-house of 1817, marooned in the middle of the miniature railway circuit, and the toilets – successfully converted out of dog-kennels!

Burwell

➤ Small though it is, Burwell is the largest village in an area of tiny hamlets, many of which have been declining in importance for centuries; some have virtually disappeared altogether.

Burwell is in a lovely position at the edge of the eastern Wolds and stands on a stream that was once famous throughout the county for its trout. In the 1200s Burwell was a significant market town, with its own gallows and an assize of bread and ale which regulated the local economy. Clearly though, it lost the battle for trade to Louth and Alford.

Perhaps this decline helps to explain an old rhyme which comments on how Burwell raised the money to repair its church:

> 'Burwell poor people
> Sold a bell
> To repair the steeple.'

The only real reminder of Burwell's market status is the octagonal Butter Cross, a unique building well worth visiting. It was built in about 1690 as a butter market, but has since been used for a number of other functions such as a dovecote, a church hall and village hall. The roof was added by Mr W. Hornsby so that it could be used for Primitive Methodist meetings.

Just to the north of the church can be seen the remaining earthworks of a Benedictine priory.

A mile south-east on the A16 is **Walmsgate**, a good example of a declining village which had probably lost most of its people by the 1450s. Its church is now gone, though some of the stone foundations are visible and can be reached by a public footpath. Alongside the A16 is a very large long barrow, the biggest in the county, and traditionally said to be the burial place of a dragon (*see Castle Carlton*).

Buslingthorpe

➤ The church of this tiny hamlet is notable for the tomb of Sir John de Buslingthorpe, a knight of the 14th century. The first of the family, Sir Richard, is supposed to have slain a local dragon near the river Ancholme and to have been rewarded by the king with the grant of 400 acres of land nearby known as Lissinglea, though the feat has also been credited to Sir John. There is a similarity between this story and the one about Castle Carlton; in both cases the 'dragon' may have been a symbol for floodwaters.

Two miles south-west, just off the A46, are the even more remarkable tombs in the church of **Snarford**. These are all related to the St Paul family who had a large mansion at Snarford. However this has disappeared along with most of the medieval village itself. The village was 'levelled' in about 1955.

Here we are in the 'clay vale' which separates the limestone edge from the Wolds, an area which has been depopulated since medieval times. Other decayed or disappeared villages in the area include **Cold Hanworth, Wickenby** and **Rand**. At **Beckering,** near **Holton Cum Beckering**, Abbey Farm is all that is left of the former village. Cold Hanworth is an excellent example of this, probably deriving its name from the 'cold' clay on which it stood; the old village can be picked out to the south of the church, which is now a house.

Wickenby airfield is one of a number in the area. It was built hastily in the Second World War – Mr Bowser the landowner met the surveyors in the morning, and at 3 pm the first bulldozers arrived. At the airfield there is a memorial to 1,080 airmen who never returned from their missions. The airfield at **Faldingworth** started life in 1940 as a 'decoy' field to divert the attention of German bombers. However, in 1942-3 it was rebuilt as a proper base, and in 1957 it became a secret site for the storing of nuclear weapons in high security, underground bunkers. Until 1972 weapons were stored here for Vulcan bombers and Polaris submarines, and because of this the base was left off the OS maps for a number of years. It was later used by BMARC, the Lincolnshire weapons manufacturer, for explosives storage.

On the main road north of Faldingworth was Gibbet Hill. The gibbet was said to have been used until the 1820s for those found guilty of sheep-stealing and highway robbery. Until the 1890s the remains of the gibbet could be seen near the lane leading to Grange Farm.

Byard's Leap

Byard's Leap is a road junction between the A17 road and the old Roman Ermine Street or 'High Dyke'. It is best known in Lincolnshire folklore for the prodigious leap made by the old blind horse Byard who was attempting to unseat a wicked witch. The witch, who was said to be powerful only between midnight and one o'clock, had been laying the district waste until a stranger offered to do battle against her with the help of the old horse.

One story says that the witch had been a beautiful young woman until she was captivated by a handsome stranger, who turned out to be the Devil himself. Both the witch and Byard died in the epic struggle, some reports saying that the heroic nag was carried back to Ancaster for burial. Where he had landed after the giant leap, his feet had left imprints on stones, but these disappeared some time ago after road alterations.

Cadney

There is a tradition that Cadney derives its name from 'island of Chad', the famous early Christian missionary associated with north Lincolnshire in particular. More definitely, from the 12th century, there was a Gilbertine priory at Newstead beside the Ancholme. The 19th century farmhouse was built on the same site and incorporates the crypt of the chapter house in its structure. Other parts of the old priory have been removed to Brocklesby.

Caistor

➤ An interesting and exceptionally historic small market town that repays a visit by the discerning. Its position on a ridge of the Wolds, with a supply of fresh water direct from springs, made it attractive to the Romans and it has been inhabited ever since. It was walled during the later years of Roman habitation, and the present church stands roughly in the centre of the walled area. It has been said that a church was started in Caistor by the missionary Paulinus in the 7th century. However, the lofty site also made Caistor inaccessible to the railways so there has been little development in the last 150 years, helping to preserve the town's character.

Caistor was noted for its 'Palmsun' sheep fair, which lasted up to four days. Consequently it once had 32 licensed houses; a measure of the town's commercial decline is that there are now only three.

Caistor played a part in the rising of 1536, when Lincolnshire people rebelled against the religious policies of Henry VIII. Hestcroft House in Church Street has iron railings around it which include a sword, said to be the one used to rally the demonstrators.

The appearance of the town owes a great deal to the disastrous fire of 1681, which destroyed many houses and killed some people. Many of the buildings around the small squares of the town date from just after this fire.

An interesting place to visit, therefore, is the home of the old fire-engine in Plough Hill; it was kept in a tunnel under the road from 1869. Close to this is one of the springs – Pigeon Spring. The name of Fountain Street betrays its connection with more springs: Syfer Spring is still extant and another spring near the churchyard ('Holy Well') once had reputed medical powers for curing diseases of the eyes. The street follows the south wall of Roman Caistor. Facing the church is some more of the wall in Church Folly. Caistor also has an underground passage story – this one is supposed to run from the 'turret' in Mill Lane to Tower House.

The church is best known for the Gad Whip, probably from a goad for oxen. This was part of a peculiar tradition involving a man from Raventhorpe holding the whip over the vicar's head on Palm Sunday: the custom is said to have started in 1536 but it was certainly disliked by some Victorians, and ceased in 1846. The whip is preserved in the church. The church also once contained a fragment of wall 'built out of human bones', said to have been brought from a Middle Eastern city; the piece is actually from Antioch, and it was thought that the blood of Christian martyrs was used to mix the mortar.

Castle Bytham

This village is one of the jewels of the Lincolnshire 'Cotswolds', the rolling limestone hills through which the tributaries of the river Glen rise. Castle Bytham is set almost dramatically on the rising ground above one of these streams, looking across to the startlingly impressive castle remains.

The remains can best be seen from beside the village pond, itself a pleasantly satisfying feature. From there the earthen hills erected by the Normans seem to dominate the countryside, yet not a vestige of the old stone walls remains. Some exciting events have occurred here, including a major siege in 1221 against the young Henry III during the revolt of William de Fortibus.

After these events the castle walls were partially ruined, but the castle was then restored and extended by William de Colevill, who had it and some land confiscated in 1265 but regained them on payment of £200. When the castle ceased to be useful, the stone walls were taken down, and pieces no doubt reused in the houses of the village. Some of the latter are impressive, including Glen House which has a round pigeon cote rivalling the one at Witham-on-the-Hill.

Reputedly there is an underground passage from the castle to Park House, about two miles away. Halfway between the two there is a sink hole in the limestone which may have

Existing earthworks of the castle.

started the tale. Apparently a Scottish piper decided to investigate but could persuade no one to accompany him, so he said that he would play his bagpipes and some locals were to follow the music on the surface. The sound suddenly ceased when he got near the sink hole and after that it was called Piper's Hole – but where did the Scotsman go?

Those who need further exercise can go to Morkery Wood, to the west. Perhaps they will be able to discover the Victorian statue of 'The Butcher', a general's horse.

A mile to the south is the hamlet of **Holywell,** where the eyes of the blind were bathed in the water which was supposed to cure them. A large hall has replaced the religious community, but it has notable gardens as a consolation.

Castle Carlton and The Restons

If ever a place can be described as a failure, then it must be Castle Carlton. Once the castle of an important knight, in 1230 Robert Lupus attempted to turn it into a market town.

So unsuccessful was this experiment, that Castle Carlton today is little more than a bump on the ground that hardly deserves its own name. Yet it is a fascinating place.

The castle was built by Sir Hugh Barde 1295 – 1302. A famous legend explains that Sir Hugh rode out to do battle against a terrifying dragon that was laying east Lincolnshire to waste. The dragon had legs encased in iron and one eye, the size of a pudding basin. After an epic struggle, and with much supernatural help, Sir Hugh killed it. The head of the dragon was sent to the king, who rewarded Sir Hugh by allowing him to change his surname to Bardolph and to take a dragon emblem as part of his coat of arms. Traditionally it is believed that the dragon was buried in the long barrow beside what is now the A16 at Walmsgate, a name which may be derived from 'worm' which was commonly used instead of 'dragon'. However it is also said that Sir Hugh killed the beast by the sea; if so he would have dragged it a long way in order to bury it. There again, some sources say that the dragon was really a wolf . . .

Sir Hugh's family later left the area and moved to Wormegay in Norfolk; presumably the name is more than just a coincidence.

A custom of the lord of Castle Carlton was to take a horn of salt from each of the salt carts that passed through the area on their way inland from the salterns on the coast.

A public footpath leads across the site of Sir Hugh's castle, part of which is covered with woodland. The village church has also gone, demolished in about 1902. So complete is the decline of the area that South Reston church has also been demolished.

Cherry Willingham

A large dormitory village, but one that has a fine Georgian church. Near the church there used to be a spring that was famous for curing weak eyesight. An iron ladle was kept at the spring for the benefit of those needing to take the water.

A mile to the west there was another famous spring at

Greetwell, called the Halliwell (or holy well). The flow of this was ruined by the ironstone mines and quarries nearby, but Greetwell is still a good example of a deserted village – the earthworks can be seen close to the church.

Cleethorpes

Cleethorpes is of course very well known as a major seaside resort, but it has a distinctive history of its own and some lesser known features.

The many stories about the origins of Cleethorpes agree on little except that it was once called something else. One story is that there was some high ground amidst the swampy coastal marsh called Mag's Highland or Meg's Island; this may explain the once common nickname for Cleethorpes people as 'Meggies', though there have been more complex theories related to the price of a ticket to Cleethorpes from Grimsby!

It has also been said that the original settlement was Itterby and that there was a church in the swampy ground between Old Clee and Humberston. Apparently this church later sank, thus accounting for the mysterious boulder that stood in the middle of the swamp. Visitors were often advised that if they stood near the boulder they would be able to hear the bells ringing.

Clee used to be famous for its 'Folly Feasts', held on alternate Sundays after Trinity. This involved much wrestling and fighting. The church floor was usually strewn with new-mown grass on Trinity Sunday.

The modern town of Cleethorpes was developed through the efforts of Sidney Sussex College, Cambridge, once the key landowners here. The college bought Itterby Manor in 1616 and the link can be seen in Cambridge Street.

The area between Clee and Scartho was once famous for springs and blow wells, though many of these were affected by the extraction of water for Grimsby. One at Isaac's Hill was noted for its iron taste and supposedly had medical values.

The worst day in the history of Cleethorpes occurred when the Baptist Chapel was bombed by a Zeppelin during World

War One. At the time the building was being used to billet soldiers and 31 were killed. The site of this can be found in Alexandra Road, though of course the chapel there is a replacement. There is a memorial at Cleethorpes cemetery. In 1916 an air-raid shelter was built just off Albert Road and Yarra Road, now used as a garage; there cannot be many World War One air-raid shelters in existence. On the same theme, the churchyard at nearby **Scartho** has a memorial erected in gratitude after the village survived a bombing, and there is a plaque in the village's 'commercial district'.

Colsterworth

◄ The area around Colsterworth is known because of its links with the great scientist, Sir Isaac Newton. His family lived in the manor at **Woolsthorpe-by-Colsterworth** from 1623, and he was born there on Christmas Day 1642, three months after the death of his father. The house is now in the care of the National Trust and the area in front of it is planted with apple trees of a type that would have been familiar to Newton – though we do not know if his famous revelation about gravity actually occurred while he was here.

Newton was baptised in the church at Colsterworth on 1st January 1643 and the Newton aisle there was rebuilt later as a monument to him; there is also a sundial made by him. After his childhood Newton spent relatively little of his life in the area, returning briefly to escape the plague but never staying for long.

Chapel Cottage, at Woolsthorpe, is peculiar in being literally that, but it is not a conversion of a former Methodist chapel, as can be found in many Lincolnshire villages. Instead it includes the nave of a medieval chapel of ease, for Woolsthorpe was never a parish and did not have a proper church.

Nearby **Skillington** is an interesting village. At one time the clergyman was the Rev Charles Hudson, a famous Victorian exponent of 'muscular Christianity'. He was a leading amateur mountaineer and also once walked 86 miles in 24 hours. He was killed with three companions in the famous Matterhorn

The church window at Skillington.

climbing expedition of July 1865, led by Edward Whymper. One of the party slipped, pulled the others from their footing, and the rope broke. Four fell 4,000 ft to their deaths, the body of Lord Douglas never being found. Hudson was buried at Zermatt, but windows at Skillington were paid for by fellow alpinists and are a very unusual feature to find in a small parish church. There is a small display about Hudson to add further interest.

It has been claimed that Newton received his first lessons at a dame school that was run in the lady chapel.

Corby Glen and Irnham

➤ Corby Glen was once a small market town but is no longer so. Apparently the stall-holders were on their way to Corby one day when they heard that a terrifying epidemic had broken out in the town; they rushed away and never came back... Despite this the village, as it then became, still had a market town's reputation for heavy drinking, once boasting nine pubs.

The town once had a small castle, to the north-west of the church. Also worth a passing visit is Round House Farm, which is really octagonal, and would doubtless be classified as a folly except it can be lived in.

For a small settlement in Lincolnshire Corby Glen is quite unusual in having a Catholic chapel. This is, in fact, substantially the one built by Lord Clifford for his house at Irnham and rebuilt in the 1820s. It was taken down in about 1855 and re-erected in Corby.

Irnham has a long history of links with Catholicism. The Thimblebys of Irnham Hall generally remained Catholics throughout the difficulties of the later 1500s, enduring fines and imprisonment. It has at least one priest's hole, entered through a step in a staircase. At one time a crucifix held by Mary Queen of Scots at her execution was kept at Irnham. In 1676 a third of all Catholics in Kesteven lived at Irnham! When the house was sold the chapel was at the centre of a legal dispute, which was resolved by moving it to Corby.

Crowland

➤ Just about the last 'town' in Lincolnshire, but one of the most important historically and a fascinating place to visit.

Deep in the Dark Ages, when the Romans had left and Britain was being attacked by plundering pagans, a young man named Guthlac came by boat to an island in the middle of the fens. He built himself a hut in an old 'long grave' and settled down to a life of quiet spiritual contemplation. His solitude was once disturbed by a terrible howling, but he was pleased to see only two demons screeching around – he had feared a pagan horde rather more. His cell was located near the west end of the south aisle of the abbey church.

During his time at what became Crowland, Guthlac was visited by Ethelbald the king of Mercia. Guthlac prophesied that he would succeed in his struggle without the need for bloodshed.

After his death, Guthlac's body remained pure for a year and his reputation as a saint was secure. His sister, who became St Pega, came to live in a cell of her own at Crowland and kept his psalter and the whip of St Bartholomew; the whip or scourge became the symbol of Guthlac. Her cell is supposed to have been at Chapel Hill, a spot just out of Crowland on the road to Postland. Later she left the area and went to Peakirk.

The monastery was founded in about AD 716, and prospered thanks to Guthlac's canonisation, but it was badly exposed to Danish attacks. In AD 850 the Danes burst in and killed the Abbot Theodore at the altar. The abbey was destroyed, then rebuilt but suffered many privations. It was damaged by an earthquake in 1117 and a fire in 1146.

In the 11th century a legend developed that helped Crowland recover its prestige. It was said that the monks were involved in a legal battle with a rapacious man over land, and the case was set to be heard at Stamford. As the rival was riding to Stamford, his horse suddenly threw him and he died of a broken neck. When his body was being carried to its funeral the cart passed a piece of land belonging to the abbey; suddenly darkness fell and there was a terrific storm. The bier broke and the corpse was thrown out into the dirt.

Another miracle occurred in 1072, during a terrible famine. A voice was heard telling the monks to look at the north corner of the monastery, and there they found two sacks of wheat and two of flour.

That the abbey maintained its prestige can be seen from the fact that Henry VI came there in 1461 to pray to Guthlac. Of course it was closed by Henry VIII and in 1643 became the scene of a small Civil War battle and three days' bombardment, during which a man fell off the tower and was killed. Crowland was strongly Royalist, and in 1643 a group of Crowland men raided Spalding and kidnapped its Puritan minister.

Part of the abbey church is still in use as the parish church and its nave lies ruined alongside. It is still an emotive site. The other famous feature of Crowland is its unique three-arched bridge. This has been the cause of much dispute, for it is positioned at what was believed to be the junction of two watercourses yet plainly this was a very complex way to cross them. A triangular bridge has stood here since AD 943, though the present one is mostly 14th century. The large seated figure was reputed to be Ethelbald, but is more probably Christ and could have been brought from the abbey. Some have suggested that the bridge was built this way to support a great cross, and it seems likely that it has some spiritual significance; perhaps a three-arched bridge is an expression of the unity of the Trinity?

Culverthorpe

➤ Culverthorpe is a tiny village on the eastern flanks of the limestone escarpment, best known for its hall and the network of country walks in the surrounding area. When visiting it, park at the 'Stepping Out' car park beside the lakes to the south-west of the main village. The best view of the hall can be obtained from the bend in the road at Culverthorpe Hollow, which looks across the lakes.

The central parts of the house date from about 1679, when they were built for Sir John Newton, the MP for Grantham and a relative of Sir Isaac. Other parts of the house were added by another Sir John in the early 1700s. The Newton family line came to an end due to a tragic accident. The only son of Sir Michael Newton was taken at the age of three months by the family's pet monkey and dropped from the roof of the family's London home. The property then passed down the female line, though a later male changed his name to Newton. The house recently featured in the BBC serial *Middlemarch*.

Close to the road that leads towards Rauceby can be seen the remains of the 1691 chapel which was re-erected on the estate as a decorative feature.

Doddington

It is surprising to find one of the county's most spectacular houses in the rather drab countryside on the western fringes of the city of Lincoln. Yet Doddington Hall is an excellent example of a late Tudor mansion, built between 1593 and 1600 by – probably – Robert Smythson. Its owner was Thomas Taylor, the Recorder for the Bishop of Lincoln.

Two tales of the hall are worth recounting. One is that a young lady who had once gone to the roof garden for a period of quiet contemplation found herself facing the unwelcome attentions of a young man. Since he clearly intended to divest her of her honour, the young lady jumped off the roof – and was saved from death by falling into the branches of a holly bush beneath.

A picture of a dog, kept in the house for many years, was supposed to be of significance. The dog apparently belonged to one Henry Stones, who had taken it out walking on a summer's day when a storm had blown up. Stones sheltered beneath a tree, but three times the dog pulled him away from beneath its branches. On the third occasion the tree was struck by lightning and a pheasant sheltering there was killed, as Stones would have been. The pheasant was duly included in the picture of the faithful dog. Stones died in 1693 and there is a memorial to him at Skellingthorpe.

Donington

Donington is a small former market town, best known for its association with Matthew Flinders, the navigator and explorer of Australian coasts who was born here in 1774. Because of this, the town gets more Australian visitors than one would expect.

A plaque in the Market Square shows where Flinders was born, but the house has been demolished. Apparently enthused by the story of Robinson Crusoe, he joined an expedition to Australia in 1791.

Flinders explored the Australian coast in 1801 in command of HMS *Investigator* and then intended to return to Britain. Not realising that Britain was once more at war with France, he put into Mauritius and was captured, spending six years in prison because of his mistake. He was buried at Woolwich, but the people of Donington erected a memorial stone in the churchyard just as if he were buried there; only a careful study of the wording provides a clue that it is not a normal gravestone. This can be found on the north side of the church.

Flinders can certainly be credited with cementing relations between Australia and Lincolnshire. Apart from naming a range of mountains and a river after himself, he used many Lincolnshire place names – for example, Cape Donington. A study of a detailed map will show the Australian coast littered with Flinders references – there is a Flinders Island and a quite separate Flinders *group* of islands!

In the church itself are various memorials to Flinders and his family, a bust of him and what could almost be called a shrine – there is much of interest. Best of all, perhaps, is the very fine stained glass window depicting Flinders and two other Lincolnshire travellers associated with Australia – George Bass and Sir Joseph Banks. Banks attended school in Donington for a while.

Also in the church is a 'hude', a graveside shelter for clergymen, and a well-preserved bier.

Just over a mile south-east is the village of **Quadring**, which appears to have moved away from its church.

Dorrington

➤ Dorrington is a good example of a Lincolnshire village which appears to have become completely detached from its church. The church stands in a dominant position on top of a low hill, whereas the village runs in a west to east direction giving access to the waters of the local beck.

According to legend, the distance to the church became something of an inconvenience to the villagers and they decided to rebuild it in a more central position near the Playgarth. Two days in a row the local people laboured at their task, and two nights in a row every stone they had moved returned to where it had started! The third night they watched to see what was happening, but nothing did, so as dawn was breaking they went off for their breakfast – only for everything to taken back again during their absence.

Presumably the Devil preferred the church to be a long way from the houses, but the same story is also told about the attempts of a Saxon thane, Tochti, to build a chapel at Chapel Hill. This seems to have been pulled down in 1698 and its stones used to repair the church. The bell was hung in an oak frame in the village to give better advertisement of services.

The church has been said to stand on the site of a pagan temple; it has also been claimed that if you look through the windows on St Thomas's night, you will see the Devil and some witches playing marbles inside! In the churchyard is the grave of a Ruskington blacksmith who was murdered between Dorrington and Digby, and there is also supposed to be the ghost of a bride who walks out of the church porch and down to the churchyard gate.

Also worth visiting in Dorrington is the North Ings Farm Museum which is clearly signposted east of the railway bridge. This remote tourist attraction has a large collection of narrow gauge railway equipment, much of it salvaged from the old potato railways that ran around Nocton. Some of the track is older still – it came from First World War trench railways. The museum is open for train rides and the inspection of the vintage tractors at weekends during the summer season.

Dunston

➥ Although Dunston is a small village, it sits within a parish boundary that extends from the banks of the river Witham to the very centre of the limestone heath on the A15. Like many of the parishes on both sides of the Heath, its boundaries were laid out to take account of the variety of soils on offer in the area and so a long, narrow shape emerged.

The most interesting building in Dunston can be found on the very western edge of the parish, several miles from the village itself. This is Dunston Pillar, a limestone pillar erected as a lighthouse in the 18th century by a man better known for orgies and black magic!

From Roman times until the late 18th century, the Heath was a wild and dangerous place. Dry, farmed only for rabbits and inhabited barely at all, it was an ideal place for footpads and highwaymen to prey on travellers between Lincoln and Sleaford. The road, mostly laid out by a Bishop of Lincoln 400 years before, was easily lost and the unenclosed landscape meant that there were few fences or walls to guide the errant traveller. The solution to these problems, is was decided, was a lighthouse.

The man who had this curious and original idea was Sir Francis Dashwood of West Wycombe in Buckinghamshire. Dashwood had a direct connection with the area as he owned Nocton Hall, though it was not his main residence, and also owned Dunston Manor, for he was actively building up his lands in this area too.

In 1751 Dashwood decided that he could help travellers on the road by setting up a lighthouse about two miles north of the old Green Man Inn. It was built out of limestone and had an octagonal lantern at the top. However what can be seen now is but a small part of Dashwood's vision, for he also decided to make Dunston Pillar into a tourist resort and a pleasure garden. Accordingly he laid out gardens, built a wall around it all, then erected two pavilions, one of which was converted into assembly rooms with a dining room.

By the 1760s Dunston Pillar had become a popular spot with the Lincoln well-to-do. It was reported that there were often as many as 16 carriages parked nearby, as the gentry of the city arrived to play quoits or to use the bowling green.

The light was used regularly until 1788, by which time the road had been repaired and much of the land enclosed so that the area was becoming less wild. After that the lantern was only lit on special occasions and in 1809 it fell down after a storm. It was replaced by a 14 foot high statue of George III by Joseph Panzetti, erected by mason John Willson. The mason's grave can be found at Harmston with this inscription:

> 'He who erected the noble King
> Is here now laid by Death's sharp sting.'

The facts of the lantern's demise contrast nicely with an alternative version of what happened. This claims that the lantern was always unpopular with local people as it was linked in the imagination with Dashwood's notorious and orgiastic Hellfire Club, and it was thought that the lantern's flame had been brought directly from Hell. Therefore the story grew that it had been taken down after Dashwood's death.

In the Second World War the Pillar became a hazard to aircraft landing nearby and so the statue and the top 60 feet of pillar were removed; part of George III now resides ignominiously in Lincoln Castle grounds and sadly the Pillar was never restored.

While in Dunston, it is worth considering Dashwood's other activities in the area. In 1766 he signed away the ownership of Nocton Hall but he still owned Dunston Pillar and the manor house. The manor was the home of Dr Willis, an unqualified 'expert' in mental illness who used it as his hospital and was meant to look after the Pillar in return.

Dashwood and Willis fell out over a land deal and the former began proceedings to get him out of his house. In the meantime, Dashwood even considered building himself a new house at the Pillar itself. However, in 1778 Willis left Dunston for Greatford and eventually fame, fortune and notoriety.

With Willis gone and Dashwood dead in 1781, the Pillar lacked a guardian. It was visited by the diarist George Byng in 1791, who commented, 'Of what use, nature or taste is this odious obelisk? It can only incur ridicule!' Byng was wrong, and today it attracts the interest of many who pass by on the A15.

The airfield that was the undoing of George III's statue was RAF Coleby Grange. This was on the west side of the A15 and the control tower is still visible; various of the buildings were on the east of the main road and can still be seen hiding in the woods near to the Pillar. This airfield opened in 1940 and the Canadian pilots there taught the station Dental Officer to fly; one day he surprised them all by landing in a Tiger Moth, telling them that he had got it from the CO at RAF Digby in exchange for a new set of dentures!

Eagle

➤ One of the most astonishing buildings in the whole of Lincolnshore can be found near Eagle – the wildly improbable house called The Jungle.

The weird frontage of the house was the creation of Samuel Collett in about 1820. He used blackened bricks for dramatic effect, and twisted oak branches were used to frame the windows – heightening the effect of Gothic mystery. Collett's eccentricities did not stop there, however, for he justified the name of the house by keeping a collection of wild animals around it, including kangaroos and buffaloes. The rear of the house was rebuilt in the 1970s.

There was, in medieval times, a preceptory of the Knights Hospitaller in Eagle. On the site of Eagle Hall may have been a 'hospital' which, by the usual tradition, was linked directly to the church by an underground passage.

The best known Eagle gravestone has been that of John Gamwell. His inscription reads:

'John Gamwell, here he lies –
Bury none by him, until his wife dies.'

However, it is commonly believed that John Gamwell was a bachelor.

Edenham and Grimsthorpe

➤ Grimsthorpe is one of the most important stately homes in Lincolnshire and is connected with one of the leading families of the county. The estate was originally built up by the Cistercian Abbey of Vaudey ('Vallis Dei'), which was founded here in 1147. This stood to the south of the present lake.

In the early 13th century the Earl of Lincoln, who lived at Folkingham, built a castle here; part of this survives in a corner of the present house as 'King John's Tower'.

The fortunes of Grimsthorpe really began to improve when the 10th Lord Willoughby married one of Katherine of

Aragon's ladies, Mary de Salinas, and was granted the estate in 1516. Their daughter married Charles Brandon, Duke of Suffolk and a close friend of Henry VIII, so they were in a strong position to take over Vaudey Abbey when it was dissolved in 1538. Brandon built a new house using many materials from the abbey, which was barely finished when Henry VIII visited in 1541. The Duchess married into the Bertie family after Brandon died, and her stay at Grimsthorpe was also briefly interrupted by the need to leave the country while Mary I was queen. Katherine was a remarkable woman with a deep Protestant faith, which she clung to despite the dangers and such tragedies as losing two sons within half an hour of each other in 1551. The house has been added to since then, principally by Vanbrugh and Hawksmoor in the 18th century.

Grimsthorpe was well used during World War II. The park south of the lake was employed as a bombing range – very carefully, for the only death was to one cow. The deer park was used for tank training. There is also a story that the army put a patrol on the castle roof and that the lead on one side was worn out by the remorseless tramp of army boots.

The castle lay within the parish of **Edenham**, and it is to that church that the visitor must go in search of the tombs of the family. There are many here, recording their advancement from Lords, to Earls and then Dukes.

Elsham

Elsham Hall has been rebuilt since 1788 and further developed in recent years as a country park. Though it may not be to everyone's taste, here at least is a Lincolnshire country house that people can actually see.

It is built close to the site of Elsham Priory, which began life as a 'hospital' (or inn) for travellers but eventually abandoned that role. There was also a Carthusian priory at **Bonby**, three miles to the north.

The nearby airfield, now cut in two by the approach road to the Humber Bridge, was first opened in 1916 as part of Britain's defences against the Zeppelin. There was a 'decoy field' opened at Great Limber when RAF Elsham Wolds was reinvigorated for the Second World War. It closed in 1947, but the old control tower was adapted into a house.

A pleasant drive from Elsham takes the traveller north through the spring line villages along the B1204 to **Horkstow**. An important find of a Roman mosaic was made here in 1796, showing Orpheus playing the lyre, and also a chariot race; it is now in Hull Museum. At Manor Farm the artist George Stubbs is said to have dissected horses in order to perfect his techniques.

Horkstow Bridge, at the end of the lane leading down to the Ancholme, is a rare example of a suspension bridge in the county – ironically, now almost in the shadow of the Humber Bridge. This one was designed by Sir John Rennie but originally the plan was for a cast iron bridge perhaps like the one at Saxby. The new design was accepted at a meeting in December 1834, so Horkstow Bridge must be one of the earliest suspension bridges in the country still standing.

The floor of Horkstow church slopes upwards rather surprisingly. This has been attributed to a need to fit the church against the hillside, but it may really be due to the creation of a vault underneath in the 17th century.

Epworth

Epworth is of course most famous for being the childhood home of both John and Charles Wesley. The former Epworth rectory is thus the centre-piece of quite a solid tourist trade in the middle of an area that would otherwise receive fairly few visitors.

Samuel Wesley, the father of the two famous sons, was rector of Epworth in the early 1700s but was by no means a popular man. The year 1705 saw him spending some time imprisoned in Lincoln Castle for debt, probably because of pressure brought by his political rivals. In February 1709 the rectory caught fire, and it has often been suggested that the fire was started deliberately. John Wesley always looked upon his rescue from the flames as a sign that he was marked out for something special in the future – 'a brand plucked from the burning'. The rectory was rebuilt and thus Epworth has

The cross where John Wesley once preached.

a genuinely beautiful building for visitors to enjoy.

The rectory was the scene of a well-documented 'haunting' in 1716-17. The ghost, generally supposed to have been an old man named Jeffery who had died in the attic, declared his presence by loud knockings and bangings. These were especially noisy when George I was mentioned in family prayers. However it was a ghost that responded to discipline, for it went quiet after Mr Wesley rebuked it for scaring his children, and even responded to an instruction to talk to him in the library rather than rattling at the nursery door.

Another place on the Epworth 'pilgrimage' is the churchyard where Samuel Wesley was buried; his tomb can be found to the right of the path that leads up to the church. It is often said that John Wesley gave his first sermons from this spot, and that he also preached at the old cross in the middle of the town.

Just south of Epworth is the hamlet of **Low Burnham**. Here is a 'holy well', really a set of springs, that was dedicated to the Redeemer. On the Feast of the Ascension the waters were said to have the power to cure deformities in children, and the site would be visited by hundreds. Crowds were enough to attract stall-holders selling gingerbread and other delicacies. Of course the fashion gradually dwindled and, in the 20th century, an attempt was even made to supply a swimming pool from the holy well, but the water proved much too cold! However there have been pilgrimages to the site in living memory, and it can be visited at map reference 786021.

Ewerby

➤ Approaching Ewerby from the A153 road, the visitor will always be struck by the gaunt ruins of Haverholme Priory, looking like a film set for *Jane Eyre* or some other tragic Gothic romance (*see Haverholme Priory*). It is a lonely spot and not one that has been inhabited with conspicuous success even by its first monks, who found the site too damp and disease-ridden and decamped to Louth.

A small nature reserve can be found at Ewerby Pond east of the village. This is an old 'borrow pit' used in the building of the Navigation and since filled with water. **Ewerby Waithe** once had several 'coffin-shaped' stones, which were reputed to have been stolen by a witch from a temple that stood on high ground – one suspects a connection with stories about Dorrington here. Apparently the witch was flying off to the fens with the stones when she was spotted by some shepherds, who fired arrows at her, causing the stones to be dropped. They are no longer visible, having been broken up for gateways.

Fillingham

➤ Fillingham is dominated by its 'castle', sitting comfortably astride the Cliff, and its lake. The castle was a result of the fashion for Gothic in the 1760s and 1770s, an enthusiasm which can also be seen at the gateway on Ermine Street and on Middle Street (the B1398). The castle belonged to Sir Cecil Wray (1735-1805), a supporter of William Pitt the younger, and beaten in the infamously corrupt Westminster election of 1784 by Charles James Fox.

Fillingham is usually accepted as the source of the river Ancholme. The exact spot is normally stated to be a pool close to Ermine Street and just visible from the road about half a mile south of the Ermine Lodge.

From 1361 to 1368 Fillingham had a famous rector, John Wycliffe, though he was often absent from the village. A leading theologian who also got mixed up in politics, he was working on a translation of the Bible into English when he died in Leicestershire in 1384. Never a favourite of conventional Catholics, Wycliffe's bones were exhumed in 1428, burnt to ashes and then the ashes were thrown into a river.

There is a large memorial in the churchyard to a hero of the Crimean War, Thomas Dalton.

Fiskerton

This small village overlooking the river Witham was once the meeting place of a manorial court. At the court the steward would arrange leases with tenants, an agreement being shown by both parties grasping each end of a six foot stick. This odd ceremony is said to have given rise to the phrase 'getting the wrong end of the stick'.

A brass memorial to a former Fiskerton priest can be found on the south side of the church. This has an unusual history, as it is supposed to have disappeared from the church in about 1863 – probably during restoration work. Some time later it was spotted by Bishop Trollope of Lincoln for sale at a second-hand shop in Lincoln High Street; the Bishop bought the brass back and returned it to the church, but two oak chests that disappeared at about the same time were never recovered.

The church appears to be oddly constructed. One explanation could be that posts and other materials from local monasteries were used in the building of it.

Like Skillington, Fiskerton has a famous mountaineer. In 1897 Stuart Vines was one of the first men to climb Mount Aconcagua (6,960 m), the highest mountain in South America.

The parish of Fiskerton extends as far as Short Ferry, where an Iron Age canoe was found in 1952. This can be seen in Lincoln Museum. Short Ferry is on a meander of the river Witham, but it is no longer the main channel since a new cut was made to improve the river for navigation in about 1810. This helped to create Branston Island, which is a detached part of the parish of Branston but more easily accessible from Short Ferry or Bardney. It is an isolated spot and is occasionally flooded to ease pressure on the lower Witham after heavy rain.

Folkingham

Folkingham is a small jewel. A decayed market town, the Georgian character of its market square is a delight and a surprise for the traveller who first rounds the corner on the A15 coming south from Sleaford. It is also a pleasure because it stands halfway between Bourne and Sleaford on an 'A' road that must be one of the enjoyable in the country for the leisure driver. Its high number reflects past importance as a coaching route rather than current traffic levels. Folkingham also stands just off Mareham Lane, on the course of a Roman road, also a delight.

The town has been of some administrative importance in Kesteven. The castle was once of significance but lost influence to Grimsthorpe, so that by 1535 it was a ruin. However it formed a useful site when Folkingham's position in Kesteven affairs led to a house of correction being built there in 1825; the exterior of this is still there and worth visiting.

The Kesteven Quarter Sessions met at Folkingham into the 19th century, and this accounts for the graceful Greyhound Hotel – virtually derelict at the time of writing. This was extended in 1789 so that meetings could be held there, and some dances and other entertainments probably also took place. But Folkingham never got a railway, and its coaching trade vanished; so too did the market. Eventually the Quarter Sessions transferred to Sleaford. The loss of past generations is the gain of the present, as Folkingham has survived with its Georgian character.

The best house is the manor house, built for the Clinton

family who once had a substantial mansion at Sempringham. It is rumoured to have been built with stones from the old castle, but as that was said to have been knocked down by Cromwell one doubts the builder would have found much there.

There used to be a 'Swallow Pit' where water levels rose and fell. The general opinion in Lincolnshire was that this depended on what the river Trent was doing.

The stocks and a whipping post are kept in the church. Perhaps they were used in 1689 on the Scottish soldiers and supporters of James II who were captured at Swaton Common during the Glorious Revolution, and were locked up in Folkingham church.

At a lonely spot on Mareham Lane, a mile and a half to the north-east, the famous Stow Fair used to be held every July under the control of Sempringham Priory. There was a chapel at the spot, which survived until 1791 at least. This quite often resulted in trouble at Folkingham, so each year three men were selected to carry halberds to check behaviour. The men were 'told' of their task by having the weapons placed outside their door. 'Stow' means 'holy place' so the fair may have had some original religious significance but it has also been suggested that it commemorated the battle believed to have taken place at Threekingham about AD 870.

Nearly two miles to the west is **Pickworth**. This is an essential place to visit, to see in the church the medieval wall-paintings with their theme of doom and retribution. Though hard to discern in places, there are some lively subjects including three men in a cauldron.

Fonaby

➤ The dominant feature at Fonaby Top − a literal name explaining its spectacular position on the Wolds − is Pelham's Pillar. This takes its name from the famous family at Brocklesby, for it was built to commemorate the planting of the Brocklesby Plantation which began in 1787. By 1828 there were over twelve million trees in what had become a forest. Designed by Edward Wilson and finished in 1848, the Pillar cost nearly £2,400 and amongst its illustrious visitors was Prince Albert. Sadly, it is surrounded with 'Private Woodland' notices.

Opposite the lodge at Pelham's Pillar is Fonaby Top farm. This has one of the most interesting legends in Lincolnshire and, for once, it is good to be able to record that the people who live there actually care about their heritage. The legend concerns the Fonaby Sack Stone. The earliest versions of the tale report that there were originally three stones piled up, and they stood in a field high on the Wolds above Fonaby House Farm. One day Christ was riding through the district on his ass, presumably on an incognito foray to check the spiritual condition of the Lincolnshire peasantry. When he saw some men mowing corn in a field at Fonaby, he rode and asked if they could spare some to feed his ass.

The men were clearly no believers in Christian charity, for they refused to give the ass grain on the grounds that they had none. When Christ asked them what was in a half-open sack, they replied that it was stone. 'Stone be it,' Christ said, whereupon the sacks of grain were transformed into stone, thus accounting for the fact that the topmost stone looked rather like the half-open top of a sack.

The stones remained in the middle of a field for generations, protected by a belief that anyone who moved them would be cursed – a belief that seems to have attached itself to many of the other glacial erratics to be found in the county. However, it was possible to plough around the stones by moving them from side to side without unpleasant effects. Eventually a farmer at Fonaby decided to move them. He harnessed his best horses to them but they would not move at all. Then he teamed the horses up with his bullocks and, after much effort, the stones moved. They were dragged downhill to the yard at Fonaby House. Within days, the animals were ill.

At first the farmer scoffed at the effects of the curse, but he changed his mind when his son became ill too. He ordered a boy with a lame mare to drag the stones back uphill, which seemed an almost impossible task, but the stones virtually walked back there themselves! Later they were moved to the hedge rather than being in the middle of the field, though this

64

apparently resulted in the deaths of the three horses involved. By about 1917 the stones had broken into smaller pieces and finding them is difficult; the skilled guidance of the farmers from Fonaby Top helped me to locate them. They are at grid reference 123033.

There is even a story to connect the Sack Stone with Pelham's Pillar. When the latter was being built in the 1840s, a stonemason took a chip from the Sack Stone in order to carve a model of the Pillar. Soon afterwards, he fell from the Pillar and broke his neck.

Freiston

➤ A straggling but interesting parish, spread between several different settlements of various sizes. The main settlement of Freiston was important enough to have a fair in the 1200s and the lord had the right to operate a gallows and ducking stool there. The fair took three days in July each year. The church is notable for the twelve foot high font cover, which had to be rescued from a ash-heap by the curate in about 1850. The font cover is said to have been carved by an apprentice as a test piece; however, when his master saw how beautiful it was, he flew into a fit of jealousy and slew the young man.

To the south of Freiston church is the site of the old priory, parts of which have been included in the house of that name. The priory began as a cell of Crowland.

The parish is festooned with tales of ghosts and underground passages. There was said to have been a passage underground from the priory to Coupledyke Hall, which started in the cellar of the former. Another passage was meant to have run from the priory to the old hospital at Spital Hill, and others to Rochford Tower in Fishtoft parish and Hussey Tower in Boston.

Spital Hill was said to be haunted by a small horse or 'shagfoal', the guardian of buried treasure. It used to appear at about midnight, and once followed a traveller who was on horseback, then leapt up behind him and almost hugged him to death. Fox Hole Lane is reputed to be the scene where a young girl waited in a tree for a lover to arrive, only to see him digging a grave to bury her in! The lover's name was supposedly Fox, so one can see the connection with the name of the road.*

A famous house in the parish is White Loaf Hall, which has a 'loaf' displayed on the finial. The house is said to be where the first white loaf was baked, but we can say more definitely that it was popular with smugglers. It has been claimed that the white loaf was 'invented' by a monk at the house, who sieved flour through his socks to reduce the roughage. The house once belonged to John Linton, who later bought the priory in 1782. He was troubled by people who stole the fruit from his orchards, and his solution was to buy a man-trap and 'bait' it with a human leg – which he bought from a local surgeon. No doubt it was an effective deterrent.

Freiston Shore is an interesting but also a rather sad place to visit, for in the period from about 1770 to 1936 it was a seaside resort. In the 1840s there were horse-races along the seafront here, though after that a period of total decline. In 1930 it was briefly suggested that the coast here could become a gigantic motor racing circuit.

* For a more detailed account of this story, see *Tales of Old Lincolnshire*, Countryside Books.

Friskney

➤ Friskney is one of several settlements located on a low bank of ground which has the sea on one side and the fens on the other, so that in Roman times and for many years after it was really an island as the '-ey' part of its name indicates.

The Romans came to the area as it provided salt, and the remains of medieval salterns can be found along the line of the Sea Bank to the east of the village. During the Dark Ages the village may have been sited further west. 'Abbey Hills' marks the site of a medieval grange.

The fens to the west were once famous for two products – cranberries and wildfowl. The cranberries were sold in large quantities to Yorkshire and Lancashire, but the trade was ended by the draining of the fen and marsh. However there is still a Cranberry Farm just to the north on Wainfleet St Mary Fen.

Wildfowl were caught using the famous decoys, elaborate systems of channels roofed over with netting, into which ducks and wild geese could be chased or scared. Friskney's most famous decoy caught 100 birds a night in its heyday and it covered 14.5 acres. Birds were also netted on the shore, but the area was notorious for its mudflats. After an Act of Parliament in 1809 a drainage programme for the fens was carried out, and the decoys were doomed. This was bitterly opposed by the local people, who had caught tens of thousands of birds a year in the fens. The East Fen drainage was one of the last great fenland schemes. In 1878 it brought an end to the last decoy, which in its later years had sent many birds to London every October and November. The sites of decoys can be traced today and are even marked on the Ordnance Survey map at Pool Decoy and Decoy Wood.

A curiosity worth seeing is the lamp standard on the south side of the church, which is made up from various pieces of medieval work. Early 15th century murals in the church were discovered in 1879; one of them shows a scene of three Jews 'stabbing' the Host, from which blood is pouring – this was part of a well-known story of the time. The church is one of several fenland parishes to possess a 'hudd' – a sort of shelter for the priest during a burial, looking rather like a sentry box.

Fulbeck

➤ Fulbeck is a delightful village on the Cliff. Its chief building is Fulbeck Hall, the home of the Fane family since it was built in 1733 – the previous house having burnt down. The house is open for a brief period each year, generally on Sundays in July.

Like all villages on the edge of the limestone, Fulbeck placed great emphasis on water supply. There was once a spring on

Fulbeck Heath, a mile to the east, that was known as Holy Well as its water was claimed to ensure longevity. In 1891 Henry Fane put up the special building for the village pump that adds charm to the village scene today.

The village achieved notoriety in 1987, when it was placed on a short list of possible areas for the dumping of nuclear waste. Luckily, Lincolnshire avoided this most fearful of indignities.

The next substantial village towards Grantham is **Caythorpe**, where various old ironstone workings can be seen. There was once a house here called Holy Cross House that was said to have the ghost of a grey lady. One version claimed that this was a farmer's wife who was murdered and hidden in a cupboard, but a more romantic tale links it to the Gunpowder Plot. Catesby, one of the conspirators, escaped to Caythorpe where his sister Lady Grey lived, but she refused to help him and so was killed.

Fulletby

One of the most elevated villages in Lincolnshire – in fact Fulletby Hill – reaching 450 feet at its tallest point, was once believed to be the highest place in the county. Not surprisingly, Fulletby Hill was used for a beacon during the Napoleonic Wars, with the village miller acting as watchman.

Despite this position high in the Wolds, Fulletby has played a part in notable Lincolnshire events. Two men from the village were probably executed at Tyburn for their part in the Lincolnshire Rising of 1536, whilst in the winter of 1830 local agricultural labourers decided to protest about their situation by planning a march on Horncastle. It was arranged that they would march to Belchford and meet other activists at the Blue Bell Inn, but when they got there they found no one else, so they had to sneak quietly home.

Less dangerous, despite his name, was Charles 'Thrasher' Richardson, a famous stirring preacher who was born at Fulletby in 1791.

Fulletby had a number of traditions. These included 'mumping', which was practised by poor women on St

Thomas's Day. They would visit the houses of the district's farmers asking for alms, usually being given corn or milk, sometimes money. The practice died out about 1890. Also dying out in Victorian times was 'rumning', a festival held in mid-July involving lots of eating, drinking, games and climbing of greasy poles.

One thing to see in Fulletby is an unusual monument in the churchyard to a 15 year old boy who died in 1865. It was designed and built by his father, including an image of his grieving mother. The inscription reads, 'So much of light, so much of joy, is buried with my only boy.'

Gainsborough

➤ Gainsborough is a historic town with a long importance due to its position on the Trent. This led to it being frequently visited by the Danes, one of whom, Sweyn, is very much associated with the town. He died here in 1013, but it has never been proved exactly where his death took place – the Pillared House, Old Hall and Thonock have all been suggested, but none of these would have existed then. It has also been claimed that his son, Cnut, was declared king at Old Hall.

The most important building in Gainsborough is Old Hall. The house is mostly 15th century, but was badly damaged in 1470 during the Wars of the Roses. Its fame partly lies in its connections with the Pilgrim Fathers, as a few of them met here in the late 1500s and early 1600s; the lord of the manor at the time allowed a group of religious separatists to worship there secretly and some of these eventually went to America on the *Mayflower*. It has also been claimed that here Henry VIII met Catherine Parr, the widow of Lord Burgh's oldest son.

The hall has seen a variety of uses over the years. Parts of it have been a factory, a ballroom, a masonic lodge, a theatre and even tenements (when it was effectively a poor house).

Gainsborough is also famous for its crossing of the Trent. For most of its history this has been a ferry, and not without accident. In December 1760 the ferry was full and ready to leave when a Beckingham man rode his horse straight onto it. In the ensuing panic the ferry overturned and six people drowned. One woman was saved as she had tied herself with string to a pig she had bought in the market; the pig swam ashore, pulling her behind it. A few years later the bridge was opened, originally as a toll bridge as the little lodges indicate. It was opened as a 'free' bridge by Mr Hore-Belisha (of zebra crossing fame) in 1932.

Gate Burton

➤ Gate Burton is best known for its 18th century hall, which has some 20th century additions. What makes it especially attractive is the landscaped park, which once extended on both sides of the main road. The best feature of the park is the 'Temple', a typically romantic 18th century feature.

The parish was also once noted for its petrifying spring, one of a number found in the Trentside parishes.

Gautby

➤ Gautby Hall was the home of the Vyners, an illustrious family, one of whom rose to become Lord Mayor of London in the 1670s. His memorial is in the church. The hall was demolished in 1872 and its stone used to repair local roads. Some of the outbuildings survived to become farm stores, and an ice-house also survived. The lake once had an island in the middle which was adorned with a statue of Charles II, but this was taken off to Yorkshire many years ago. The overall effect is a sad one, perhaps a telling memorial for the transience of Lincolnshire country house life.

At **Minting**, a mile to the east, was a Benedictine priory founded in about 1129. The earthworks can be seen behind the pub.

Gedney

➤ Once one of the bigger parishes in Lincolnshire, in area, if not in people, Gedney measured 11,614 acres of land and a further 59 acres of water, so huge because fenland reclamation had extended the boundaries over successive generations. The original Gedney, on the silt bank near the main road, grew several daughter settlements as far away as Gedney Hill. The name of the latter may appear to the visitor to be something of an exaggeration, but in the fens a few feet can make an enormous difference. For many centuries the area was important for salt-making as it stood on the edge of the sea, but that trade has now gone. The hummocks that remain from the medieval period can still be seen at Gedney Dyke.

Gedney was a manor belonging to the Abbey of Crowland, which kept a manor house about 100 yards north of the church. There was rumoured to have been a 'covered way' connecting the house with the chancel of the church and the broken arches on the north side of the chancel were meant to be 'proof' of this.

Gedney church is unusual in having the beginnings of a stone spire, but has to make do with what has been called a 'little lead spike'. It has been said that the spire was never finished due to problems with the church's foundations – it was supposedly built on a raft on the peat bog. In days gone by you could stand in the porch, jump up and down, and feel the floor vibrate. Now the ground is drier, you would need to be very heavy indeed to achieve this! Around the tower is a building join, reputed to mark where work stopped during the Black Death and then restarted years afterwards to a different design.

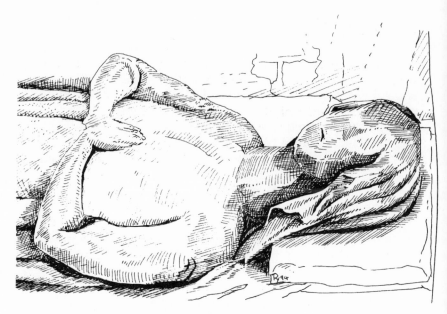

Is this Molly Grime?

Glentham

➤ In Glentham church a worn and damaged medieval tomb of a woman was once the centre-piece of a strange local tradition. Through a bequest granted in the Middle Ages, the sum of seven shillings was allowed each year to pay seven old women to collect water from a spring called the Newell Well on the Seggimoor Beck west of the village. They were expected to carry it to the church and to wash the tomb, which was known as 'Molly Grime'. This was to occur on Good Fridays and the old women were each allowed a shilling, but this also had to cover the cost of the mourning clothes that they wore.

The tradition was clearly associated with the events of the first Good Friday, and its meaning becomes more clear when it is realised that Glentham church was once dedicated to 'Our Lady of Sorrows'.

Glentworth

Lincolnshire has a number of romantic ruins, among which can be counted the remnants of Glentworth Hall. It was built in the late 16th century by Sir Christopher Wray, who had become Lord Chief Justice in 1574 under Elizabeth I. In 1586 he took part in the trial of Mary Queen of Scots, and died in 1593. His splendid tomb can be found in the church.

In the 1750s the Earl of Scarborough decided to make Glentworth has main residence, and an ambitious rebuilding scheme began. However it was never finished and the present house is but a shadow of what was intended.

In the 19th century Glentworth was nearly the scene of the death of one of England's leading 'sportsmen', Lord Henry Bentinck, who was reputed to spend £40,000 a year on his racing stable. When trying to ride under an archway near the village, a blind wall caused him to panic, and he would have been killed had it not been for his top hat.

Glentworth also has some Roman remains, as a large Roman villa is known to have existed close to the hall. It had a bath house too. Just to the north of Glentworth is **Harpswell**, once home of the Whichcote family. Some earthworks are all that remain of another Lincolnshire's country homes.

Grantham

Grantham is the most important town in the south of the county. Although it has grown immensely since the railway arrived in the 1840s, it still has many attractive features and is dominated by the wonderful spire of St Wulfram's church, 282 feet high. Supposedly this was built in one go in order to outdo Newark, where the people also built a tall spire but needed to have a rest part of the way up. The church is dedicated to St Wulfram, and some relics of him were once kept there; Grantham celebrated St Wulfram's Day with a special fair on 15th October.

Another famous building in the town is the Angel and Royal Hotel, dating from the 15th century, though there has probably been an inn or 'hospital' for travellers on the site since the 13th century. There have been many famous visitors to the inn, including Richard III who is said to have sealed the death warrant of the Duke of Buckingham while staying in the King's Chamber in 1483. Charles I reputedly stayed there in 1633, while the stone figures outside are believed to be Edward III and his Queen.

Less fortunate in how commercialism has treated it is the 'George', now a shopping centre, through a fairly tasteful one. Charles Dickens stayed there in 1838 and thought it was 'the most comfortable inn I have ever put up at'. Part of the site was where Newton lodged when a pupil at school in Grantham; there is a plaque at the school to commemorate this.

In Grantham and around it are many pubs with the word 'Blue' in their name. These date from the early 19th century when there was political rivalry between the Manners family, Dukes of Rutland from Belvoir, and the Brownlow family of Belton. Although the Manners family were Whigs, their colour was blue and the pubs were expected to indicate this allegiance. It is said that the rival faction named a pub the Blue Ass as a protest! At one time there 13 blue inns, such as the Blue Lion and the Blue Ram. The Blue Pig is still one of the town's most attractive inns and, while on the subject, we should mention The Beehive with its famous sign.

The Conduit, in the market place, is also interesting. The Grey Friars came to Grantham in about 1290 but had problems with the water supply, so in about 1318 they got permission to bring water from the springs at Great Gonerby. The conduit was rebuilt in 1517 with the trademark of the Grantham woolstaplers placed upon it. In 1655 an order had to be made against people for 'annoying' the conduit by washing their clothes there. Between here and the Angel and Royal is Coal Hill, which got its name from what was sold there, as no coal has yet been discovered under Grantham.

Grantham used to be famous for its gingerbread. Travellers on the Great North Road used to be sold Grantham Whetstones near the George Hotel, but in about 1740 a baker started to make Grantham Gingerbreads. The secret recipe was passed down to the firm of Catlins', whose restaurant in the middle of Grantham is unoccupied at the time of writing. Perhaps this is a tradition which could be revived?

Grantham is now famous (or infamous?) as the birthplace of Margaret Roberts, who became Mrs Thatcher the Prime Minister. The former Roberts' family shop can be found in North Parade, now known as The Premier restaurant.

Great Gonerby

➤ Until the 1960s heavy lorries laboured up and down the hills of Great Gonerby, which stood on the Great North Road. It has improved immensely since Grantham bypass opened, and is now much quieter.

The most famous tale connected with the village is to do with the church clock, and explains (supposedly) why Great Gonerby people are called 'Clockpelters'. Young men were meant to stand at the village pond and throw stones at the church clock; anyone who managed to score a 'hit' was adjudged to have reached manhood. The alternative version relates that children at the school used to pelt the clock with stones or snowballs in order to stop its hands moving, and thus to extend their playtime.

Greatford

➤ An attractive and interesting village, best known for the curious garden ornaments dotted about by Major C. Fitzwilliam, once the owner of Greatford Hall. In the 1930s he had a business supplying stone garden furniture to London department stores and seems to have used 'his' village to exhibit his designs.

A number of them can be found, so it is best to park near the pub and walk around seeing who can spot the most. Very obvious are the two giant coronets in the gardens of the cottages opposite the pub, but similar designs can be found even in the gardens of quite new properties. The lane up to the church, which passes the hall, is lined with them. One is a flower tub embellished with rather developed young ladies

The giant garden ornaments at Greatford.

(or maybe they are just goddesses!). Two of Fitzwilliam's coronets can also be seen in the unlikely setting of a factory entrance at Carlby, on the A6121.

The visitor to Greatford should certainly visit the church because it contains a number of interesting monuments connected with the family of Dr Willis, the famous 'mad doctor' of George III.

Willis came from Lincoln and, after a time at Dunston, set up his 'medical practice' around Greatford, looking after mentally disturbed patients who were brought to him on the strength of his reputation in dealing with the king. Willis seems to have used Shillingthorpe Hall and Greatford Hall at various times. An amusing story has been told of Willis at Greatford, which apparently dates from 1807, just before his death. It was claimed that 'Sir Henry F . . .' was riding through the district when he fell from his horse and lost his reason for a few hours.

When he began to come to his senses, he found that he had been helped to a fine house in the neighbourhood, where an old gentleman looked after him.

After a little while Sir Henry was judged fit enough to come downstairs for dinner, where he found the kind old gentleman and 16 other men – no ladies anywhere! Nobody was allowed any wine, but all else seemed normal until the old gentleman left the table. Then, one of the other men turned to Sir Henry and asked, 'By what misfortune, sir, have you been unhappily trepanned by the unfeeling man?' The man then told Sir Henry that he had been there for 15 years.

The others also told Sir Henry some frightening stories, such as that his host was a magician and that other men had been shot for trying to escape. However the old man then reappeared and asked Sir Henry to accompany him, assuring the astonished gentleman that the others at the meal had been quite mad and that his name was Willis. No doubt Sir Henry was overjoyed to be allowed to resume his journey.

Great Ponton

➤ Anthony Ellis, a rich merchant of the Calais staple – the wool trade – is strongly linked with Great Ponton. In the early 1500s when there were a number of problems threatening the orderly conduct of the trade, Ellis (or Ellys) sent his wife a cask labelled 'Calais Sand' and told her to put it in the cellar until he returned. Doubtless he did this because of the difficulty of sending packages safely, for when it was eventually opened it proved to contain his fortune in gold!

Ellis and his wife had no children, so in 1519 they used their money to build an impressive church tower in their village. The family's arms can be seen near the west door. He also built what is now the Old Rectory, which has a unique set of 16th century wall paintings.

On the tower is a weather vane in the unusual shape of a violin. According to tradition, a wandering minstrel who gave money to the church asked that a violin should be his memorial.

Stoke Rochford, a mile or two to the south, is an almost

The church with the violin weathervane.

dramatic landscape of steeply sided valleys and woodlands. It makes a fine setting for the house, built in a park which was once famous for its spring. This spring was said to be so powerful that it could operate a watermill.

Grimsby

The origins of Grimsby are lost in antiquity, but by tradition the town has claimed to have been founded by the fishermen Grim in the Dark Ages. He is an important character in the saga of Havelock the Dane, one of the most popular of medieval tales. A connection with this tale was Havelock's stone, an ancient boundary stone that once stood in Brighowgate but which doubtless had nothing to do with Havelock.

Grimsby, a town largely of the 19th and 20th centuries despite its ancient origins, has few things to see of note. However it has had some interesting characters. One of these was Parson Leek, who was meant to care for the souls of Grimsby and also **Holton-le-Clay**. He rarely went to Holton, so the people complained. Leek's response was to tell them that they were safe to sin as much as they liked, since 'the roads are so bad the Devil himself could not go' to Holton. Another time a summons was issued against him for debt, but when an officer arrived he was shown Leek lying in a coffin. Supposing him to be dead, the debt was discharged, but Leek was mysteriously resurrected soon afterwards.

Ned Pearson was the parish sexton, nicknamed 'Old Bluebeard'. He was said to be capable of predicting a death and would hang around a likely house for some time when he expected the Grim Reaper to call. Not that the church had all Grimsby's people in fear; behaviour in the town was so bad at one time that the church authorities petitioned the Bishop to be allowed to hold their services at the safe time of 2 pm on a Sunday, rather than the perilous time of 6 pm when heavy drinking was in progress.

As Ned Pearson was so much concerned with the graveyard he probably knew of of its most curious grave – that of a watchmaker. Its inscription runs:

'Here lies one who tried to equal time
A task too hard, each power too sublime,
Time stopped his motion
Overthrew his balance wheel,
Wore off his pivots
Though made of hardened steel.'

Many people think that Grimsby stands on the river
Humber, but of course it is really on the Freshney and this
is commemorated by the name of the shopping centre. There
was once an island in the middle of the Freshney inhabited
by a hermit-type called Billy Croft, whose only friend was a
raven. His hut was washed away in a gale so he emigrated
to Clee Marsh but his final house was an upturned boat.
Perhaps Croft would have known of Ducking Stool Haven,
at the bridge over the Freshney; this was used until 1780.

Grimsby was notorious for its corrupt elections. Any
freeman of the town was allowed to vote – providing he was
married to the widow or daughter of a freeman. This strange
rule was said to have originated with Elizabeth I, who was
concerned that the women of Grimsby were so ugly that no
one would marry them.

An MP elected in 1669 complained that votes had cost him
'£300 in ale and £52 in buttered ale'. By the 19th century the
elections in the town involved much ingenious bribery and
a fair amount of violence. Clever canvassers got rival
supporters drunk and then packed them on to the next train
for London, and clever candidates suddenly discovered that
voters owned precious items that they desperately wanted to
'buy'. One Grimsby voter sold his canary for £50 and another
a teapot for 80 guineas. Getting elected was expensive.

Despite all this, Grimsby was once a small Lincolnshire town
with its own semi-rural traditions. There was a Whitsun
festival which centred on the lost church of St Mary; there
were sports in the churchyard and 'Robin Hood's Arbour' was
set up there and the maidens gathered contributions. The
churchwardens brewed 'whitsun-ales' which apparently they
sold in the church.

The other major event in Grimsby life was the Hock Tide
festival, two weeks after Easter. On the first day of this the

women stopped all the streets around the market with cord and 'ransomed' any men they caught; the following day the roles were reversed. This festival was supposed to celebrate the defeat of the Danes in 1002.

The most prominent building in Grimsby is the tower at the Docks. This was built in 1851-2 and is 309 ft tall, so at present it is the highest building in the county, apart from the Belmont TV tower. Less well known is that it is a copy of the medieval tower at Siena in Italy and stored water for the hydraulic system that operated the dock gates.

Haceby

➤ Here is a settlement where even the word 'hamlet' seems to credit it with excessive grandeur! Indeed, if one were looking for a place to typify the most hidden village in Lincolnshire, Haceby would surely be a contender. It can be approached only by narrow single track roads with dangerous bends and, when arrived at, could easily be mistaken for a farmyard – of the fairly derelict variety!

The church is, of course, redundant, but this seems no excuse for the apparent state of collapse of everything around it. The only activity left here seems to be at Moat Farm, which takes its name from a substantial moated site to the south-east of the church. It is hard to imagine that in the 1500s Haceby was a thriving village with 40 households.

Hainton

➤ Hainton is famous as the home of the Heneage family. The substance of the house dates from 1638, but it has been much rebuilt and the grounds landscaped by 'Capability' Brown. There were disastrous fires in 1919 and 1924 and part of it was removed in 1956. A well-known Heneage in more recent times has been George, who was an MP at various times for Grimsby and Lincoln. He was also unusual in being a Roman Catholic and built a Catholic chapel for the hall in 1836. The family kept a Catholic priest at Sixhills for many years from the 1600s.

Surmounting George's achievements was Edward, whose political career took him to become Chancellor of the Duchy of Lancaster and who was made a baron in 1896.

Visitors to Hainton used to enjoy a trip to Benniworth Haven, a walk through woodland past two fish ponds just to the west of the river Bain. The area can still be crossed by public path, and it is possible to believe the reports that its beauty was much appreciated by royalty.

Halton Holegate

It is said that the 'Holegate' part of the name derives from a deep cutting through sandstone on the road from Firsby to Spilsby, properly known as 'Hollowgate'. A bridge was eventually put across it to make access between the church and the rectory much easier.

The village has unproven connections with some major events. Richard Holegate, a Tudor Archbishop of York, is said to have been from the village; he was imprisoned by Queen Mary but paid a ransom for his own release. It has also been claimed that a parishioner named Parker was involved in the Gunpowder Plot, and that the rector of Halton gave evidence against him.

A more definite connection is with Thomas Clay, a bachelor of the parish and churchwarden in 1658 and 1661-2. A ghostly story suggests that the death of a Halton parishioner is foretold by the appearance of 'Clay's Light'. Clay used to live in a 'hut' near Halton Fenside, in the fens along the Steeping river, and would walk to church over the field path rather than the road. In his will he stipulated that his coffin was to be carried to the church by this route, but his wishes were ignored. On the eve of his funeral a light was seen to cross the fen from his hut to the church, and ever since it has been said that Clay's Light appears near the house of a dying villager.

Harlaxton

➤ Harlaxton Manor is one of the glories of Lincolnshire and, although owned by an American university, it is open regularly for people to enjoy. It was designed by Anthony Salvin in 1837-45 for Gregory Gregory, to replace the old manor. The Gregory family came into Harlaxton when Anne Orton married Gregory Gregory (they kept to the same name!) in 1738. According to the story, she was the heiress to the estate but disappeared as a child and Gregory was sent to look for her in 1730. One version relates that she had been kidnapped by gypsies and he found her singing a Lincolnshire lullaby at Spitalfields in London. Another version claims that he went into a shop to buy gloves and found her working behind the counter. Either way, he married her and made the estate his!

The village has other interesting stories. In Tudor times a gold helmet studded with jewels was found in the village and given to Katherine of Aragon; she is supposed, rather ungraciously, to have sent it to Madrid.

There used to be a stone about 50 yards from the old manor house labelled 'Bill's Leap, 1633'. The tradition attached to this was that Charles I passed by in 1633 and 'Bill' was so excited about seeing the king that he made a big leap of joy – there was a second stone seven yards away, from which he presumably began his daredevil flight.

A will of 1826 left money for the bell of Harlaxton church to be rung in the morning and evening. This must have been one of the last times that this common local tradition took place in a village.

Haverholme Priory

➤ Haverholme today is a gaunt ruin of a house, standing out across the fields from Ewerby as if a relic from *Jane Eyre*. Just off the Skegness road, there are obvious opportunities for tourist development like Witley Court in Worcestershire, but the site is surrounded by forbidding notices.

The priory is best known as a house of the Gilbertines, an

order not averse to living in lonely situations or damp and unhealthy ones – as in this case. However it was the Cistercians who came here first, but they did not like it and sold out to the Gilbertines when they moved to Louth Park in 1139.

It has been claimed that Haverholme kept a hermitage on the edge of the fen where Thomas à Becket hid in 1164 during one of his disputes with the king.

One of the duties of Haverholme was to maintain transport links and drainage on the fens. In 1316 the prior was in trouble for not keeping a foot ferry going at the 'Wathemouth' – possibly across the Slea at Ewerby Waithe. The monks were in trouble again in 1360 when Alice, daughter of John de Everingham, fled from the priory but was recaptured. She told the bishop that she had never taken full vows and was held against her will, so he ordered her release.

After the Dissolution, Haverholme was adopted for domestic use, being finally rebuilt in 1830 for the Earl of Winchelsea. The estate was put up for sale in the 1920s but did not attract a buyer, so much of the house was demolished in 1927. What is left is well worth going to see; it is approached across a bridge over the New Slea, itself a fine structure to find on a country lane, and through a gate at what is now a car park for local walkers.

While visiting Haverholme, it is worth walking along the Slea to Haverholme Lock. This sylvan scene will soon be reanimated as plans progress to revive the Slea as a navigation.

Haxey

Haxey is most famous for the Haxey Hood Game, a survival of a medieval folk tradition that is celebrated on the twelfth day after Christmas each year. The game is said to have originated when a great lady dropped her hood in some mud and enjoyed the sight of the local peasantry struggling to collect it so that they might claim a reward from her. A tradition of getting local youths to flounder in the mud was thus begun, with the denizens of Haxey and **Westwoodside** rivalling each other for the capture of the prized 'hood'. Various extra features have been added to the ceremony each year, including the bizarre 'smoking the fool', which starts it all off at the mounting stone outside Haxey's impressive church.

Haxey also has a tradition of well-behaved bell-ringers. This dates back to 1785, when rules were first hung up in the base of the tower. They declared that a bell-ringer who wore spurs, a hat or a greatcoat would be fined 6d, while those who started a quarrel must pay a shilling.

Visitors to Haxey often approach from the south, crossing what was once a dank fen either side of the river Idle. Here was 'Parson's Cross', though more properly known as Parting Cross. Traditionally this was the place where the Duke of Norfolk parted from his Duchess in 1397, having been challenged to battle by Henry Bolingbroke, who became Henry IV in 1399. The duke ended on the losing side and was banished by Henry, never to see his duchess again. He died in Venice of the plague.

In the 1620s trouble returned to Haxey when Cornelius Vermuyden began the drainage of the fens or 'carrs'. Areas like Haxey Mere, which was three feet deep even in summer, had provided fertile opportunities for local people to augment their diet with wildfowl, eels and fish. So strongly did they feel about their 'rights' in this respect, that a 14th century deed which they believed supported their case was kept enshrined in the church. The draining of the meres and carrs meant profit for friends of Charles I and local people were incensed.

In 1628 they launched a riotous assault on Vermuyden and his Dutch workmen in an attempt to stop the scheme. Vermuyden's men armed themselves and a local man was shot dead. Violence continued for several years afterwards, though Vermuyden had the backing of the king and clever lawyers. In 1642 much of the reclaimed land was deliberately flooded in order to keep Royalist soldiers out.

In February 1741 fire devastated Haxey. Breaking out at night, in three hours it destroyed 62 houses. Local people were terrified and were 'driven naked into the fields'. The fire was supposed to have been started in a flax workshop after an employee had been sacked. Others claimed that it was caused by a lad in the flax workshop trying to burn a spider as it climbed up the wall.

Heighington

➤ Does Heighington have a church or not? The answer, perhaps, is 'not really'.

Heighington has always been rather in the shadow of **Washingborough**, which may account for the fact that by the late 1500s its village church had fallen into disrepair. In such state it fell into the clutches of Thomas Garrett of **Canwick**, a local adventurer with interests in fen drainage, who may even have used the building as a store house for a while. However, in 1619 he decided to repair the church and it became a chapel of ease, not having the same status as a parish church.

When Garrett died he left money to Heighington, **Branston** and Washingborough parishes but not to Canwick. This was allegedly because he had been refused permission to walk his dog in Canwick churchyard. His chapel survived, though in 1865 it was partly adapted into a school. It continues to look very church-like, and has now been rededicated to turn it back into a 'proper' church.

Hemswell

➤ Hemswell is one of the small villages that line the Cliff, usually sited where there was a spring of water. The name of Hemswell betrays this origin and a field near the village, known as 'Well field', was once famous for its seven springs. One of the springs was known for its ability to cure eye problems, but nowadays many of Lincolnshire's springs have been lost due to over-extraction of ground water. Nowadays the village is better known for its maypole.

Most people who visit Hemswell never really get there, for they are generally more interested in visiting the old RAF camp at Hemswell Cliff, which is now an antiques centre. The base was known as Harpswell in 1918, but was reopened as Hemswell in 1937. It attracted notice more recently, when it was used in 1973 to house Ugandan Asians made homeless through the policies of Idi Amin. Several of the buildings have been converted into almost a 'department store' of antique shops, though attempts to make the base an air museum have met with less conspicuous success.

Heydour

➤ A tiny but interesting settlement that is almost hidden by the low hills surrounding it. The church here is locked, but the key can be obtained locally and is well worth visiting as it contains the monuments of the Newton family from nearby Culverthorpe Hall. Several of these are impressive.

Leave your car outside the church and walk along the lane to the west. The first point of interest will be the old rectory. Church Lees House, which dates from about 1800. Set above the door is an ancient carved figure of stone, supposed to be the only remnant of Heydour castle. This certainly makes it worth including in a tour of Lincolnshire secrets for, like its monasteries, Lincolnshire's castles have a habit of vanishing!

A little further along the lane, near some more recent cottages, can be seen the earthworks of the castle, mostly visible as earthworks of the ring and bailey type. It is an interesting comment on how the hamlet of Heydour has declined in importance since Norman times.

Hibaldstow

➤ This is a large village just off the A15, Ermine Street; the village is said to have grown as traffic abandoned the old decaying Roman road, using what is now the B1206. There was a Roman settlement in the area near Staniwells Farm, to the west.

The name of the village has caused it to be linked with Hybald (or 'Higebold') of Lindsey. He may have been the Abbot of Bardney, while the 'stow' in a place name often denotes a holy or burial place. It has therefore been assumed that Hybald was either martyred by being burnt here, or had some form of mission station in the area.

The old RAF field at Hibaldstow is notable in that its control tower was 'recycled' in an unusual manner – it was made into a house!

Holbeach

A significant Fenland town of some interest, Holbeach in the past has been a major market town and the cause of some rivalry between landowners, and also of bad feeling towards the monasteries that were dominant landowners in the Fens. A dispute with the Abbot of Crowland in 1189 involved several thousand people.

There are two popular stories associated with Holbeach. In the mid 18th century up until 1783 a feature of the town was three old friends who liked to play cards at the Chequers Inn – until one of them died. The night before his burial they had a few too many drinks, then forced their way into the church where his coffin was resting. They set up the cards on the altar and disinterred their friend to act as dummy in a game of whist. What happened next grew in the telling, for it was said that when it came to the dummy's turn to play, three demons appeared, each claiming one of the card-players, and everyone vanished in a puff of smoke! In fact the story of the card game seems to be true, though the demons are probably not, as the participants were known to be in the district for some years afterwards. One of them, a man called Watson, became a doctor but committed suicide in about 1805. He was buried off the Spalding road, a mile from the church.

Another tale is that some young farmers stopped overnight in Holbeach on their way back to Boston from Norwich. After a few drinks, one of them discovered his cart had flown up on to the roof of the church – for there it was, and he could not think how it got there. What had happened, of course, was that some friends had dismantled it, carried the pieces on to the roof and then put it together again!

The church itself is impressive, but the curiosity is the north porch. It has two round towers as if a castle, and it has been suggested that the towers were actually brought from a real castle, Moulton claimed as a local candidate.

The town is known among historians as the home of William Stukeley, an 18th century antiquarian who recorded details of many medieval buildings that are now lost. Stukeley Hall stood on the site of his house until 1993.

Christie House, in the marshes to the north, was the home of the founder of Glyndebourne Opera. At Holbeach Hurn, Sir Arthur Thistlewood is supposed to have lain in hiding while plotting the Cato Street Conspiracy to murder the entire government. There is also a tradition that King John once hid from his rebellious barons in Washway Road . . .

Horbling

➤ The most notable feature of Horbling, an attractive but unspectacular village, can be found in the suitably-named Spring Lane. This is an old well, built in 1711 at a cost of £9.15s.5d. In an unusual arrangement, the water rises almost imperceptibly from a central cistern and feeds into three

The ancient well or spring.

adjacent troughs. The way that water flows endlessly from an apparently motionless pool has always had some form of mystical appeal to human nature, so coins can still be found in the cistern; but earlier this century it was also common for people to place photos in the water!

A blend of tea was once devised especially to suit the waters of the spring. Another type of drink is available at the Plough – this is a bit unusual in that it is a pub whose freehold is owned by the parish!

The council houses in Horbling are built on a site where prisoners of war were once housed in World War II.

Priory Farm, two miles to the north-east, owes its name to a Gilbertine priory that was once here. It has been claimed that the monks had the duty of praying for travellers as they made their often-perilous way across the medieval fens.

Horncastle

The crowds making for the coast skirt the edge of Horncastle, hardly knowing what a treat they are missing. The town is a wonderful example of how English market towns used to be before they became over-developed or swamped by chain-stores; it is also famous for its antique shops.

Horncastle was a Roman town and may have been known as 'Banovallum'. Parts of the Roman wall can be seen in Dog Kennel Yard, south-west of the church, and in the foyer of the library.

The Romans were attracted partly by the defensive site in the angle of the rivers Bain and Waring. The rivers have been a mixed blessing for the town, as proved by the height of the 1960 flood marked on Old Bank Chambers. The 1920 flood accounted for a row of cottages at the junction of Bridge Street and West Street.

In days gone by Horncastle was most famous for its fairs, especially the Horse Fair when traders came from throughout the country to strike deals. At one time there were three fairs, one of which had been 'transferred' from Market Stainton. The fair was especially popular with gypsies and was surrounded with the usual boisterous and drunken behaviour.

Many private houses used to double up as licensed (or unlicensed) premises for the duration of the fair, hanging a sign outside on the hedge. The Horse Fair reached the knacker's yard in 1948.

In the parish church can be found a collection of scythes. There used to be about 50 of these, but now rather fewer, and they are believed to be relics of the 1536 Lincolnshire Rising, when the men and monks of the county unwisely decided to challenge Henry VIII's religious policies.

Evidence can be found in the town of the Horncastle Navigation, which by a law of 1792 was empowered to improve the river Bain for barges. It opened in 1802 and helped the town to achieve quiet prosperity in pre-railway days.

In the market place can be seen the Stanhope memorial. This stands on the site of the old lock-up, which was once also the butter house! Another lock-up was built nearby, though very cheaply – a sweep managed to escape by digging under the wall which had no foundations.

The Whelpton almshouses owe their funding to a chance discovery. Mr Whelpton found an old recipe of a Boston doctor for curing stomach and kidney diseases. He tried it out on his wife and found that it worked, so the mixture was used to make a fortune from the London trade. The almshouses were founded as a memorial to the wife.

Number 30, Boston Road is a house with a curious decoration – the death mask of the last man to be executed in the town for burglary. This was 'Tiger Tom', who in 1829 paid the ultimate price for a career of robbery and terrorising, which culminated in an attack on Halstead Hall near Stixwould in February 1829 for which three were executed in Lincoln; another one was 'thrown overboard' while being taken to Australia. 'Hangman's Corner' was close to the Drill Hall site and was apparently popular at the time of the Horse Fair.

Two famous Horncastle residents are worthy of mention. Sir Joseph Banks, the botanist, had a town house in the High Street. William Marwood was a local tradesman with a cobbler's shop in Church Lane; he became England's public executioner from 1860 to 1883, although it is said that his wife never knew the reason for his periodic absences. He executed over 350 people at £20 a day. For a time he lived at St Mary's

Square, marking the house with a lion stone in 1877. Marwood's last home in the town was at 64 Foundry Street (although it has also been quoted as 149).

Marwood used to stop off at the Portland Arms pub in Lincoln, and was supposedly the victim of an attempted poisoning by its Irish customers after he had been to Dublin to hang the Phoenix Park murderers. The pub used to have a collection of his ropes, but these were lost in a rebuilding.

Horsington

➤ Horsington is claimed to be the birthplace of Arthur Thistlewood, who was the leader of a conspiracy in 1820 to murder the entire government as they met for a dinner party. The members of the Cato Street Conspiracy were surprised in their lair and a government agent killed in the struggle. Thistlewood and several other conspirators, including one from Sleaford, were executed by hanging and then beheaded.

Thistlewood's father is believed to have been a grazier from Tupholme near Bardney, and his mother the daughter of a Horsington shopkeeper – they were not married. Much of Thistlewood's life is shrouded with mystery; for example, it is claimed that he married an heiress in Lincoln then gambled away her fortune, but no record of the wedding has been found.

The village church was rebuilt on a new site in Victorian times, replacing an old church to the south-west. This church followed a common pattern of having been built on a pagan site, which was apparently used by the ancient Britons to light fires in November to celebrate their new year. This follows a similar pattern to Dorrington, for example. A parish chest that used to be kept in the church contained Horsington's equivalent of the psychiatric profession – a brass collar used to restrain the insane.

A lonely farm to the south-east is Poolham Hall. A small part of a medieval domestic chapel can be seen near the farm.

Hough on the Hill

A nicely sited village in the undulating countryside north of Grantham. The prominent site was fortified with a motte and bailey, but it would seem this never grew into a proper castle. The motte now forms part of an orchard while the bailey seems to encircle the church.

Hough church has some Anglo-Saxon parts. The tower seems to have been built with fortification in mind and, unusually, has the staircase projecting out from the wall.

There is a steep drop from the churchyard to the road. Beyond it was an Augustinian priory, of which only earthworks remain. It has been claimed that King John spent his last night here in 1216 before going on to die in Newark.

Within the parish is the source spring of the river Brant. This contains iron and was once reputed to have medical value.

To the south-west is the prominent Loveden Hill, a very significant place in earlier times. It was the meeting place for the wapentake (administrative division) of Loveden in Anglo-Saxon times and was an important burial place in the Dark Ages. When the site was excavated in 1955-9 evidence was found of both burials and cremations from the 6th and 7th centuries. Some of the urns had the swastika emblem then symbolising the sun, or good luck. A footpath skirts the edge of the site.

Huttoft

Huttoft once stood on the coast, but man has gradually pushed the sea to the east although his battle against it has not been without its problems. There is now a car park and picnic site at Huttoft Bank, a mile and a half to the east, which is one of the best places in the area to see the 'petrified forest' of ancient trees that are scattered along the coast and visible at low tide. They are reckoned to be 4,500 years old.

The village is notable for the magnificent carved font in its church. It includes the Virgin holding a bunch of lilies, a child with an apple and various apostles with 'sprouting' hair. It has been suggested that the figure with a scourge on the shaft is Lincolnshire's Guthlac.

In the actual village is a rather curious sight – an old windmill which has been provided with battlements!

An old Huttoft tradition was the celebration of 'Clerk Thursday' as a holiday after Ash Wednesday. This caused problems after the introduction of compulsory schooling as local children refused to attend on that day.

Ingham

Ingham is a large village on the Cliff, centred around an extensive green. Several skeletons have been dug up from the green, presumed to be Danes. Some of the skeletons found in the area were discovered with their legs crossed and facing downwards.

The village pond was once the cause of a bitter dispute between a landowner and the parish over rights to its water. The landowner wanted to charge local people for access to it.

A famous inhabitant of the district around Ingham was the highwayman Dick Turpin. He preyed on travellers along Ermine Street and once stopped two ladies in the parish of Ingham. Having been robbed of every coin, the ladies pleaded that they had no money left to pay for room at an inn. Ever a ladies' man, Turpin handed back to them two sovereigns, declaring 'I, too, am poor, ladies.'

Ingham is one of a number of sites where an airfield was built in World War II. When this was opened in 1942 Cliff House was converted into the officers' mess and Cliff House Farm was left rather isolated in the middle of the airfield. The control tower survives.

Ingoldmells

There are few palm trees in Lincolnshire, but Ingoldmells has been able to boast of one right outside its church.

The legend of the palm tree relates that the squire's daughter, Charlotte, fell in love with a servant named Jonah.

They used to meet secretly at the church but one night the squire passed by and realised what was going on. He disapproved and the young man was sent away to sea and died in a shipwreck. His friends arranged to have the body brought back and it was buried and a palm tree planted to grow over it, presumably to commemorate the area where he died. Charlotte died of a broken heart soon afterwards.

Irby upon Humber

➤ Firstly a misnomer – Irby is *not* on the Humber, though it is closer to the Humber than the other Lincolnshire Irby.

At the west end of the village is Irby Dales Farm. Here, in a prominent position facing the road, is an unusual building – an octagonal 'horse gin' (meaning engine) which was used to pump water after it was built in 1855.

North of the village is Irby Dales itself. This is connected with a local ghost story. A plumber from Grimsby had been working in the country and was walking home in the dark, past Irby Dales, when he passed a gateway and heard a terrifying scream. The man panicked and ran all the way to Laceby. Several years later he was close to the same spot when he met a shocked and terrified farmer: the man had just found some human bones by the roadside at the bottom of the dale.

The bones turned out to be those of a young woman. A few years before there had been an engaged couple in Irby who had suddenly left. The accepted version was that the man had kept delaying their wedding but eventually a date had been fixed. The previous evening the couple disappeared and did not return. Later a note came from Hull saying that they had decided to go off together. Two years afterwards the man returned, saying that his 'wife' had left him – but really he had left her, dead, in Irby Dales.

Irby in the Marsh

 Irby is a straggling hamlet along the Spilsby to Firsby road. There is little to see here but it is the setting for an intriguing tale, though there seems a lot of confusion as to details. The tale, dating from the 16th century, concerns a young lady named Mary Irby who fell in love with a young man who was disliked by her family. The young lady hid in a remote and forgotten room of the family castle, her location known only to an old gamekeeper who had the key to the room and supplied her with food. One day the gamekeeper was shot in a fight with poachers and, unable to escape from her cell, Mary Irby died of starvation. Afterwards it was said that her ghost haunted the castle. When it was demolished and the stones used to build a more modern residence, Mary continued to haunt the building.

The most confusing aspect is that Irby is not known to have had a castle, though the story could refer to one of the moated sites in the area.

Kirkby-cum-Osgodby

Osgodby, Kirkby and Kingerby form a line of small settlements – three in hardly more than a mile.

In **Osgodby** is an unusual Catholic chapel claimed to be the earliest one in Lincolnshire. It is unusual in that the chapel is at the first floor level and was built above a house in 1793 after a change in the law allowed Roman Catholics the freedom of worship. It was built by the Young family, one of a small number of Lincolnshire families who clung to Catholicism.

Osgodby has no church, for it is part of Kirkby-cum-Osgodby, suggesting a unifying of the parishes at some stage in the past when depopulation was a problem. In the churchyard of Kirkby is buried the Proctor of the Lincoln engineering firm, Ruston, Proctor & Co. This is now European Gas Turbines, but the 'P' of Proctor still survives on a tall chimney there.

In **Kirkby** church are the tombs of the Wildbore family.

Legend relates that the family got their name because a knight fought a battle with wild pigs near the church, and that this accounts for the 'rough ground' there.

Kingerby is tiny – but interesting. The old house here stood on a mound within a moat crossed by a drawbridge, close to the site of a Roman camp. The site was used for a castle in medieval times, and the house was rebuilt there in 1812 – and later much reduced by fire. The site has been the home of the Young family for a long while and, because of their Catholicism, is associated with tales of hidden priests. Not fully explained was the discovery, in the early 1800s (possibly during the rebuilding of the house?) of two men, buried in sawdust with mosaic rings on their arms.

There was a chalybeate spring west of the village that was supposed to have medical powers (at map reference 045915).

One of the piers at the entrance to the hall is supported by a stone, dated 1451, from the Bishop Bridge – the crossing of the Ancholme two miles to the south-east. This seems most likely to have been brought to Kingerby in the early 1800s when the Ancholme Navigation was built. The Navigation helped make Bishopbridge something of a minor industrial centre, but the Navigation was never extended to Market Rasen or to join the Barlings Eau and thus remained a backwater.

Just over half a mile west of the church on the road going to South Culham, Thomas Young of Jesmond Farm put up a cross on a tree in 1855 to record his thanks that his cattle had escaped cattle plague. Apparently his brother. James of Kingerby Hall, was a hard drinker who did not care about religion – his cattle suffered badly. Between this and the church are the almshouses, founded in 1675 but now falling into ruin.

Kirkstead

➤ Kirkstead was once one of the most important monasteries in eastern England, but now all that remains on the surface is a pillar of rock and the chapel of St Leonard. The Cistercians built their abbey on this site in 1187.

The last remains of Kirkstead Abbey.

However, they were not always popular and by Edward I's time the abbot was detested for blocking up local roads and the Witham for his own advantage. He also hanged people on a gallows at Thimbleby. A later abbot was heavily involved in the Lincolnshire Rising of 1536, for which he was executed.

A persistent tale about Kirkstead is that there was once an underground passage between the abbey and Tattershall. This may have derived from the monks having diverted a stream through a culvert. There is a story that a man and his dog once went into the 'tunnel' to try and trace it; the man took a bugle with him so that he could give a blast at regular intervals to let his friends know how he was progressing. However the bugle sounds ceased suddenly; the dog ran back out but the man was never seen again – so be careful when you are exploring the site.

The pillar that remains is the south-east angle of the south transept, the rest of the stonework having been gradually removed to use in later buildings like the Old Hall. This gaunt pillar stands rather isolated in a field that usually contains sheep or cattle; thus it is easy to lend credence to the tale that in about 1800 animals grazing around the stone suddenly rushed off in terror. Seconds later there was a loud crack and a large chunk of masonry fell to the ground.

Some distance beyond the pillar can be found St Leonard's, a medieval gem though often locked. This was a chapel used for visitors to the monastery.

Kirton-in-Holland

➤ Once a market town, Kirton was eclipsed by the growth of nearby Boston and now has almost the status of a suburb. It has a huge fenland parish, stretching right across to Kirton Holme near Hubbert's Bridge.

The area was central to the anti-drainage riots of 1768, when a crowd gathered at Hubbert's Bridge to stop the drainage scheme that threatened their way of life. Some marched on Boston, where they tore up legal papers and threatened officials. Others gathered at Kirton, but their plan to burn Boston was frustrated by the presence of army units. Sporadic violence continued through 1769 as the work progressed, and John Woods of Swineshead was shot through a window and killed. A house called Clay Hills was also attacked, but a man inside fired at the assailants and killed John Tunnard. Attempts to prosecute the rioters proved difficult as the fenland communities closed ranks.

Now the fens to the east and west of Kirton are quiet, undisturbed by strong passions, and Kirton has almost lost the atmosphere of a fenland town altogether. It has had one famous native, though, in Sarah Swift, who was born at Blossom Hall in Kirton Sheldyke in 1854. She became matron at Guy's Hospital and was a founder of the Royal College of Nursing in 1916.

Between Kirton and Boston is **Wyberton**, where occasional visitors are directed to have a look at 'Wybert's Castle'. This is misleading, for the site was really just an ordinary moated house of which there were hundreds in Lincolnshire in medieval times. A house on the A1121 west of Boston has preserved relics from Wyberton's railway halt, which are visible from the road.

Kirton-in-Lindsey

Kirton is an attractive little town, beautifully situated on the Lincoln Edge though once much more important than it is now. This is shown to rather sad effect in its market square, which is surrounded by few shops of any significance and spends most of its time as a quiet car park. Yet there is character a-plenty here, and the town contains much of interest.

Starting at the Market Place, the dominant building is the bank, though it started life in 1897 as the town hall. However, much of it had a life even before that, for some of the materials had been used previously to build the town gaol in Queen Street in 1791-4. The existence of this gaol reflects the fact that Kirton was once a town of some administrative importance, and parts of it survive as The Priory to the west of the Market Place.

At the top of Spa Hill a rather gaunt and forbidding house is, in fact, the old police station. Not surprisingly, it too used

The police house and whipping post.

recycled materials from the old gaol – perhaps explaining its severe appearance. On a small green outside this building is a rare survival of a harsher punitive climate – the town's whipping post; try it for size!

Kirton-in-Lindsey railway station must qualify as one of Lincolnshire's lost or hidden places. It seems that this station is hidden even from British Rail (or 'Regional Railways'), for its current train service consists of a few trains on Saturday and none at all for the rest of the week. From the station can be seen the south portal of Kirton tunnel, which was castellated extravagantly when it was built in 1849.

On a minor road to the north-east of Kirton can be found the deserted medieval village of **Gainsthorpe**. This is one of the best of those romantic sites accessible to the public, and there is a small space for parking. It seems to have been deserted by 1616, and by 1697 had attracted a number of colourful stories, one of which claimed that it had been a city populated by thieves and robbers but was destroyed by local people. There were rumours of a castle nearby and it has also been claimed that it was a 'Roman city', but its real situation became more certain when it was one of the first of such sites to be surveyed by aerial photography in the 1920s.

Langton by Spilsby

A small hamlet just off the A16 in the 'foothills' of the Wolds. Just to the north of the village can be found the 'Spellow Hills', a prehistoric long barrow much dug over in the past by amateur archaeologists. In fact it has been dug up so often that it tends to be referred to as *three* barrows – hence the misleading name – there may have been others.

The village is supposed to have given its name to Stephen Langton, Archbishop of Canterbury in the 13th century; however, this honour is due to Langton-by-Wragby, a victim of the Lincolnshire multiplicity of confusing place names.

One person we can more definitely connect with this Langton was Dr Johnson, who was a friend of the Langton family. One day Johnson went for a walk from the house up a steep hill, which we might assume to be along the valley to the north; once at the top of the steep slope, he literally 'rolled' back down again! The house in which he stayed in 1764 was replaced in 1822, but, because of structural problems, demolished just over 30 years later. Even the replacement hall has been demolished now, though a few decaying outbuildings survive to help the visitor's imagination. The farm known as Old Hall is not really – it was used by the Langtons during the replacement of their collapsing house in the Victorian period.

The village has been owned by the Langton family since the 12th century, and it is very rare for a family to still live in the place from which they derive their name. It is still common, though, for people in Lincolnshire to have names derived from local places – Louth, Metheringham and Tupholme can all be found, among others.

One sight worth seeing is the Round House, an estate cottage with a thatched roof, to the east of the church. There was a similar cottage beside the Aswardby road, but it burnt down many years ago.

Lea

➤ Knaith Park, near Lea, was the site of the Cistercian nunnery of Heynings. One legend has it that, in the 14th century, the rector of Lea took a close personal interest in one of the nuns. This interest developed to the point where he dressed her in a green gown and they ran off together.

In 1643 Lea was the scene of much excitement when Gainsborough was captured by the Parliamentary forces. The Earl of Kingston was sent away by barge but the barge was shot at by Royalists and the unfortunate Earl killed. In July the Royalists surrounding the town were attacked by Cromwell on a low, sandy hill at Lea. In this battle General Charles Cavendish, the Royalist commander, was killed by a sword in the ribs while he was trapped in a quagmire, at a spot later known as Cavendish's Bog. It can be found on the north side of Lea, between the road and the river.

Just south of Lea is the hamlet of **Knaith**, a delightful little settlement beside the Trent. Near Knaith Park Farm many spear heads and battle axes were found in the 19th century, leading to the assumption that the area once witnessed a titanic struggle against the Danes. Knaith Park is one of the county's most remarkable landed estates and is architecturally unmatched by anything else in Lincolnshire.

Leasingham

➤ Leasingham is the last settlement on the A15 before it begins the long and lonely journey across the Heath to Lincoln. The village has several features of interest, including small stone wellheads in Moor Lane and Rookery Lane. In Rookery Lane also is a stone memorial to Richard Myddleton, who was denied burial in the churchyard in 1835, due to doctrinal differences, even though he was the village 'squire'. Near to the stone is a memorial he put up for his favourite horses.

To the west of Leasingham the road to Newark follows high ground as it climbs towards Byard's Leap. There was once an inn along here at Windmill House, a haunt of highwaymen. The highwaymen were also active at Dunsby Hollow on the Lincoln road, one of the few places where that road curves.

Dunsby, a mile north of Leasingham, is worth a visit and motorists should park in the layby on the west side of the road as it descends to the bottom of the Hollow. Dunsby, on the east side of the road, is a classic example of a deserted medieval village.

Hardly a mile north of Dunsby is another deserted medieval village, **Brauncewell** ('Bronswell'). The site is easily studied as it is crossed by a footpath and the way in which the stream was diverted can be seen. A survival here is the church, the subject of an extraordinary local paper headline – 'Sheep Vandalise Church', which says something about the character of this part of the county. Both these villages seem to have undergone rapid decline in the 1500s, probably due to agricultural change.

At Brauncewell Grange to the west is an old 'horse gin' of about 1800.

Lincoln

➤ A whole book could be written on 'Hidden Lincoln', so all that can be done here is to make a few personal selections. The High Bridge is one of Lincoln's best known sights as it carries on its west side a row of 16th century shops. Opposite, though, is an open space on the bridge which is now just used for people to rest. Few of them are aware that this was the site of a medieval bridge chapel dedicated to St Thomas à Becket and built between 1173 and 1200. It was demolished in the 18th century and replaced by an obelisk, which was itself demolished in 1939.

The High Bridge forms the first stage on the water route from the Fossdyke to Boston. However it is erroneous to think that therefore the waterway has been in continuous use since Roman times. In fact the Fossdyke has been out of use on several occasions, sometimes for long periods. There were problems throughout the 1600s and 1700s until in 1741 control of the Fossdyke was sold to Richard Ellison; this was at about the time that the Brayford Pool froze solid and an 'ox roast' was held on it. Ellison and his son made great progress, followed by improvements to the Witham up as far as Stamp End Lock where a celebratory dance was held in 1771.

All this left the problem of High Bridge, where there were disputes over tolls and problems with the depth of water. In the end the City was forced to allow improvements to the river beneath the High Bridge, which was actually floored with wood. Before the work started, wooden planks were laid and a dance held under the bridge! One presumes that these planks were actually a form of scaffolding erected to help the work.

Most tourists who walk between uphill and downhill Lincoln use Steep Hill, but the alternative is Greestone Stairs and this is a delightful route leading down a narrow passageway and through a postern gate. The name probably derives from the old English word 'greesen' meaning stairs. Before the construction of Lindum Hill, the Greestone (perhaps we should leave out the 'Stairs'?) continued down to Monks Road.

The postern gate is part of the medieval defences of the cathedral close. The gate was actually needed in 1727 when the Dean ordered the taking down of the spires that once stood on top of the cathedral's towers. A crowd in the town decided to stop this and began to threaten violence, so all the gates around the cathedral were closed – except Greestone Stairs. The crowd forced through this and attacked the house of Rev Cunnington, making him 'dance' on the green outside. The situation was saved when the chancellor provided free beer for everybody and the Dean agreed to forego demolition of the spires – which eventually went in 1807 without further trouble.

Close to where Greestone Stairs joins Lindum Hill is the former Christ's Hospital Girls' School, now part of the Art College. Close to it was a house called the Greestones, which was the staff boarding house. During the Second World War a Hampden bomber crashed here, and one of the school's language teachers died in the resulting fire. In fact such crashes were very common during the war years – eleven died in 1943 when an RAF plane crashed on Highfield Avenue.

Monks Road does have a connection with monks, but one doubts that many of Lincoln's visitors wander down this unattractive road to discover it. It was once called Baggerholmgate, which sounds rather enticing in comparison.

The Monks Well off Monks Road gave its name to nearby Spa Street. The water was said to be good for 'female illnesses' and 'flabiness of the muscles', but would not keep its powers and so had to be drunk straight from the wellhead.

The well gave its name to a church here that has disappeared – St Peter at Pump or St Peter at Welles. The church fell down and there were no parishioners to repair it. However there are some visible remains of the Black Monks Abbey in Monks Road.

A building in Bailgate used for craft fairs and similar events is the Assembly Rooms. The most famous events here were the Stuff Balls, a tradition which began in Alford in the 1780s. This was a time when the Lincolnshire wool trade was in a desperate state, and the Ball rules stated that all ladies had to wear a gown of Lincolnshire wool to stimulate trade. It became an annual event and in 1789 was transferred to Lincoln as the Old Windmill Inn at Alford could not cope with the crowd. The insistence on a wool gown was dropped in 1803

– ladies had to promise to buy some gowns instead.

Outside the historic city, the Birchwood housing estate has swallowed up the site of RAF Skellingthorpe, though a memorial has been put up to commemorate it. The name 'Manser Square' is also a good clue – for Manser was a Flying Officer who won the Victoria Cross in May 1941.

Little Bytham

➤ Little Bytham is dominated by the main railway line of the former Great Northern Railway, which now carries Inter-City expresses from King's Cross to Edinburgh. The most important event that ever happened here is to do with the railway, and is commemorated in the name of 'Mallard House' close to the viaduct.

In 1938 the London and North-Eastern Railway was running a series of high-speed trials on the line between Grantham and Peterborough. The long descent from Stoke Summit towards Peterborough was ideal for such runs, since it had the advantage of both gravity and straight track. On July 3rd, A4 Pacific locomotive *Mallard* was selected to haul the high-speed run, passing Stoke signal-box at about 75 mph. By Corby Glen it was over 100 mph and it passed through Little Bytham at just over 120 mph, later peaking at 126 mph before developing severe mechanical problems that prevented it getting to Peterborough.

Mallard's record-breaking trip has been acknowledged as the highest speed ever reached by a steam locomotive in the world, so it is pleasing that this event continues to be marked so close to where it happened . . . but nowadays 126 mph is an everyday event for the new electric trains.

Long Sutton

➤ Long Sutton is a large fenland town with a number of 'daughter' settlements. In its church, in the north aisle, is the tomb of John Bailey, a surgeon who was murdered in 1794. Within the parish there is Pop Bottle Bridge, which had the top of a bottle of pop built into it.

Dick Turpin the highwayman is said to have lived at Long Sutton when he was 'retired', under the pretence of being a gentleman horse-farmer named Palmer. In fact he was stealing most of the horses and was eventually caught and executed at York. It is also believed that Turpin stayed at an inn behind the post office.

In **Sutton Marsh** is a farm called King John Farm. It is reputed that King John lost his treasure here in 1216 when caught by the tides en route from King's Lynn to Swineshead. Nobody has found it yet, so it might still be there... John of Gaunt had a moated house in Long Sutton which stood southeast of the church.

Sutton Bridge stands on the river Nene. The original bridge was opened here in 1831 with a movable centre, being replaced in 1850 by a Robert Stephenson design. In 1894-7 a new bridge was built by the Midland and Great Northern Railway at a cost of £80,000 and this allowed trains and road traffic to use the same structure. When the railway closed, the track was taken up and the space used to increase road capacity but the bridge you drive over today is still, essentially, a railway bridge. In the village is an ordinary street named 'Royal Close'; it earned this name recently when Prince Charles visited one of its denizens, an interesting old poacher named McKenzie Thorpe.

To the north of the main road in Sutton Bridge is a golf course. This was once a large dock! The dock opened in May 1881 with a delivery of Norwegian Pine and a chorus of *Rule Britannia*, but within two months it had collapsed due to the instability of the silt which it was built on. To repair it would have cost as much as the building of it in the first place, so it was all abandoned. Clearly this must count as the 'hidden' harbour of Lincolnshire.

Sutton Crosses once had two medieval stone crosses. There is also a cross known as the Ivy Cross or St Ives Cross at **Sutton St James**, positioned on a fenland bank once thought to be Roman. There is another cross at Manor Hill Corner, probably 14th century. The church at Sutton St James is unusual in having no nave – just a tower and chancel; the rest fell down in the 17th century and was never rebuilt.

Sutton St Edmund is about eight miles from its 'mother' settlement. Thus it was provided with its own church in 1795, which has retained a delightful 18th century interior.

Lutton, just over a mile north of Long Sutton, was once the home of a well-known drunkard called Redhead. According to tradition, Redhead worried that after his death people would visit the churchyard and say 'Here lies drunken Redhead'. So he ordered that his coffin be interred upright after his death which was in 1770! There was a memorial to him on the south-east wall of the church.

Straddling the border between Lincolnshire and Cambridgeshire are the Tydds. **Tydd St Mary** and part of **Tydd Gote** are in Lincolnshire. It has been suggested that they are named after the tide which once reached here, but a more likely explanation is that the name derives from teat – reflecting that they stand on slightly raised ground. However the tide idea did give rise to a dreadful pun – that Tydd Gote was really 'Tide-Go-Out'. It has been claimed that Nicholas Breakspear, the only Englishman ever to become a pope, was once rector of Tydd St Mary – a doubtful claim. Vanished from Tydd St Mary is Dunton Hall, a large mansion rebuilt in the mid-1700s for £12,000. Its owner left it to his great-nephew, who promptly demolished the lot! In its place now is an early 19th century, more modest farmhouse.

Louth

➤ A classic English market town, justly famous for its church and also for the way in which it has preserved the character of what English towns were like years ago.

The town is dominated by the steeple of St James, a majestic 295 ft high and finished in 1515. However St James was not the original parish church, for there was one in the north-west part of the town that was abandoned in about 1529 and put to other uses, such as a school, until demolition in 1756. It is said that in 1818 a man drank ten pints of beer, then climbed the steeple, danced a hornpipe on the top and then stood on one leg on a pinnacle. The tip of the present spire is not the one that was danced on; that was struck by lightning in 1843 replaced the following year. The remains of the old tip can be found in the rectory garden, where it once formed part of a collection of follies put together by Wolley Jolland in the 1780s.

Close to the church door can be found a salutary reminder of Louth's part in the 1536 rising against Henry VIII's religious policies, which which the Louth clergy and local people were much involved. No doubt the memorial acts as a gruesome reminder to the present incumbent of Louth to keep his behaviour under control!

Louth has been familiar with disaster. During the plague of 1651 the town lost 747 people in a year, including 500 in the months of July and August. A temporary market was used a mile outside the town on the Louth road. In more modern times, the town is known for the Louth flood of 1920, which drowned 23 people when the swollen waters of the river Lud burst through the town. There is a sad memorial to the event in the town cemetery: 'Let not the waterflood overwhelm me, neither let the deep swallow me up'.

Louth Park is an old Cistercian abbey, founded in 1139 after the monks rejected Haverholme as too unpleasant. It became one of the most important monasteries in the county, and even possessed a substantial waterway called Monks Dyke which brought in water from the Lud.

In Broadbank is a four and a half ton glacial erratic boulder, which was once outside the Blue Stone Inn in Mercer Street – where it was painted blue, of course. Louth stands on the Greenwich Meridian, the course of which is marked in Eastgate. Also in Eastgate is the manor, which was once visited by Lord Byron and where the old stables are reputedly haunted by the ghost of a groom.

Also in Eastgate is one of Louth's lesser known treasures, The Priory, now an hotel. This was designed and built by a local antiquarian, Thomas Espin, in 1818 when Gothic styles were fashionable. He collected several fragments from the ruins of Louth Abbey to create a suitable effect in the garden, and also designed his own mausoleum there in which he was interred in 1822.

Louth had its share of 'holy' wells. There was a well in Aswell Street and another at St Helen's while a mill in Bridge

Street had 'several' wells in its cellars which were supposedly holy.

The main beauty spot in Louth is Hubbard's Hills, a delightful country park formed where glacial activity caused the diversion of water channels in the Wolds area. The property here was given to the public in 1907.

Just over a mile to the west of Louth is Thorpe Hall at **South Elkington**, the home of the Bolle family. During the siege of Cadiz in 1596 Captain John Bolle was put in charge of some prisoners, including a beautiful Spanish lady. She fell in love with him and showered him with presents, but was heartbroken to discover that he was already married. She is said to have become known as the 'Green Lady' and to have taken to a nunnery before dying in 1606. She was buried at Haugh.

Mablethorpe and Sutton-on-Sea

Mablethorpe, Trusthorpe and Sutton form an almost continuous urban belt along the Lincolnshire coast. The coastline is studded with the remains of ancient trees, 4,500 years old, which were studied by the famous Lincolnshire botanist and scientist Sir Joseph Banks. He found examples of birch, oak, and fir trees in 1796.

This is a reminder that the coast here is constantly changing and visitors to Sutton will be aware how the centre of the town is dominated by the coastal defences erected to prevent any repetition of the disastrous floods of 1953. Sutton was inundated and the Beach Hotel cut off; cars floated down the main street and the Bacchus Hotel, supposedly an old smuggling inn, was isolated. There were many deaths in the area, especially of elderly people trapped inside bungalows.

Fragments of the coast have disappeared completely, such as the church of Mablethorpe St Peter's, which was lost in the 1540s. Banks was told that he would be able to see its remains at low tide, but was unconvinced.

The most important local family were the Fitzwilliams. One off them is connected with the legend of Earl's Bridge, an unremarkable spot on the A1104 west of the town of

Mablethorpe. It is said that one knight was guarding the bridge when another tried to cross and they fought each other. The battle ended with them both dead together on the bridge; one was taken to be buried at Maltby and the other at Mablethorpe St Mary's. This is meant to explain the tombs of knights in the two churches, between which lies the disputed bridge. Sadly, though, the Maltby knight seems to date from about 1300 while the Mablethorpe one is supposed to be Thomas Fitzwilliam, who died in 1494 (his helmet also survives); still, it makes a good story!

Another story of the Fitzwilliams is that the French raided their home at Mablethorpe Hall (now a nursing home) and took away a young heir. The family had to pay a huge ransom, forcing the sacrifice of some of their estates. The hall was also garrisoned by Royalists during the Civil War.

A curious pub name in Mablethorpe is the Book in Hand. This is believed to have originated from the figurehead of a wrecked ship, which was set up as the sign of the pub. There was once also a Pie in Hand pub, which was no doubt more appealing to Mablethorpe's less cultured day-trippers.

Manthorpe

The former Bowthorpe Park, south of Manthorpe, is famous for the 'Bowthorpe Oak'. This ancient tree is 39 ft around and hollow inside. Various claims have been made about what has happened within. Among them are that 39 people managed to stand upright together within it, and that 16 managed to sit down to have tea. The children from Manthorpe chapel also had their annual treat inside, but that seems more believable. The Bowthorpe Oak can be seen from the main road, at a distance of about 350 yards, and not far from the farmhouse.

The disused railway tunnel at **Toft** is now a nature reserve.

Markby

Markby is little more than a church, yet what it has is very special – the only thatched church in Lincolnshire. It is a tiny and rather attractive one, consisting of only a nave and chancel with no tower or chapels.

Around the little church, especially to the south-east, can be seen the earthworks of the old priory which was founded for the Augustinians in about 1160. In medieval times the parish had its own church, but this was allowed to fall down when the local people made do with part of the priory's church. Of course, when the priory was closed down by Henry VIII, Markby was left without a church and so the people built themselves one out of the remains of the priory. Timbers were used to make an oak chest in the little church and its pews were probably made from the timber of a wrecked ship. The font seems also to have come from the priory and the church's bell was probably the monk's refectory bell. The chancel arch is obviously a relic of the priory too.

Originally the little church has a tiled roof, but this was replaced with thatch in 1672. The Priory Farm is also said to have been built from the remains of the priory.

There was also an abbey at Hagnaby and, as it stood in marshy ground a mile to the north, it needed extensive earthworks to make such a site habitable. The earthworks are still visible, though the stone of the buildings has long since been reused elsewhere.

There is a legend that if you ran three times round the church at midnight and hammered a nail into the door you would see a ghost. This is the reason for so many nails in the door!

Market Deeping and Deeping St James

➤ These two townships stand on the river Welland and the boundary of Lincolnshire. Both have charming river frontages and are worth a visit, having many attractive limestone buildings. Separating them is not easy – the boundary between Market Deeping and Deeping St James actually runs between two shops.

The Market Place at Deeping is small but attractive. It must have seemed even smaller when a row of buildings called Middle Row stood in the middle – this was removed by public subscription in 1847.

The church at Market Deeping is dedicated to St Guthlac, revealing the influence of the fenland saint so close to Crowland. In the church is a wall memorial to William Goodale who died at the age of 110. The church has also been noted for its 'Kings and Queens' window, a piece of Victorian celebration – it includes Etheldreda (the saint), David, Solomon, Edmund of East Anglia and . . . Victoria.

The most notable building in the town is Market Deeping's Old Rectory, a huge building dating back to the 14th century. Traditionally it has been considered to be part of 'Market Deeping Priory', but it seems unlikely that there ever was one!

There was a priory at **Deeping St James**, a Benedictine one founded by Baldwin Wake of the local family that later lay claim to Hereward. The Benedictines left behind a huge church, which now serves the parish; in the past it was referred to as 'Kill Parson', as its enormous size meant that parsons tended to wear out from trying to preach there. It is one of a number of fenland churches to preserve a 'hude' – a graveside shelter to protect the parson during funerals. In view of the church's reputation perhaps he needed it.

Priory Farmhouse, near the church is said to have been built from the stones of the priory. The Boathouse was built in the 17th century for barges to unload in; the open front has been filled in with a window.

The curiosity of Deeping St James is the village cross. In a bizarre mixture of possible uses for a structure, it was converted into the 'lock-up' in 1819 when it was provided with three stones seats, and later still had a street lamp attached to it.

West Deeping has no features of exceptional interest yet makes a delightful combination of buildings and scenes. There is an attractive water mill and a cottage with a sundial dating from about 1700, seemingly these are a feature of the district.

Towngate, on the north side of Market Deeping, was once the scene of rather informal horse-racing as is shown in the name of the local hostelry – the Winning Post Inn. Various attempts were made to maintain the interest in these races – in 1849 they included bicycle and tricycle events.

Market Rasen

➤ Market Rasen, **Middle Rasen** and **West Rasen** form a string of settlements along the little river Rase and its tributaries. The former is the most important nowadays and, because of horse-racing, by far the best known, though it was Middle Rasen that was the original market town. The rivalry between the various parts of 'Rasen' was reflected in a Shrove Tuesday football match between Market Rasen and Middle Rasen. People along the route used to board up their windows and many of the protagonists fell into the beck.

A street in Market Rasen named Dear Street is said to have got its name as an unwitting buyer managed to pay for it twice over.

The most famous vicar of Market Rasen was William Storr, for the unfortunate reason that he was murdered in 1602. Storr got involved in a dispute over land and a prayer of his was interpreted as a comment on his adversaries. One of these, Francis Cartwright, the only son of the lord of the manor, denounced Storr as a 'scurvy, lowsie, paltry priest' in the Market Place. He said he would 'cut his throat, tear out his heart, and hang his quarters on the maypole.'

Cartwright believed that a later sermon of Storr's was an attack on him, and at eight o'clock one morning killed the vicar with a sword. Storr lived long enough, with a severed leg, to forgive his assailant, but Cartwright was released on 'very slender baile'. Cartwright fled abroad but his friends were able to purchase a pardon from James I. Storr's wife sued him, and attempts to bribe her were unsuccessful.

On his return to Britain, Cartwright was attacked by four men, one of whom he killed. This resulted in him having to make a confession before the Archbishop of Canterbury. Later he got into a land dispute with a man in Grantham, who died; Cartwright received a year in gaol for his crime. In 1621 he wrote a full account of his eventful life.

West Rasen used to have a small wood called Ding Dong Land. This was left to the parish to pay for the ringing of the church bell at night in winter, a variant of a common Lincolnshire tradition. The woods were apparently destroyed in the Enclosures. The village is also notable for its 15th century packhorse bridge.

Middle Rasen used to have two churches and still has two churchyards. This was because it was divided between the monks of two different priories, each of whom maintained their own church. St Paul's church was demolished in 1860.

Messingham

➤ Messingham was a village that once enjoyed an extensive and active community folklore. Christmas tended to last three weeks and featured many social visits from villagers to each other's homes. On these visits a yule log, peat bag or 'cassan' would be burnt. Shrove Tuesday was commemorated by the usual cock fights and football, while at Easter the Hall Garth was the scene of dancing. There was also a big feast at Trinity.

Like most villages before the enclosures, Messingham had a common on which the villagers could graze their animals. Sheep were usual, but there was a Messingham tradition that each flock should contain at least one black sheep to ensure good luck.

Good luck could also be obtained, at one time in the 1800s, by stealing a piece of thatch from the roof of an old witch named Nanny Moody. If burnt, the thatch was supposed to ward off wicked spirits. Some unkind local youths once forced the old lady into their pub, where they made her sit on a chair covered with pins as some sort of 'test' of her witchcraft.

In 1750 a house at West Common was used by two notorious highwaymen named Dixon and Hilton. One was eventually executed at York for highway robbery and the other never dared to return.

The village cross once stood in the centre of the village with the stocks nearby. When it was removed a sycamore tree was planted there and became known as the Cross Tree. It is said that John Wesley preached at the spot, but the tree was replaced in the 19th century.

A popular old story about Messingham concerns a traveller who was passing through the village on a Sunday. He met three men sitting at a stile near the church, and was somewhat surprised to hear them shouting, 'Come to church, Thompson'. The traveller began to question them and discovered that they were a tinker, a carpenter and a shoemaker, and were acting as substitutes for church bells as the village did not have any. The traveller was so concerned about this that he agreed to pay for three bells if the men would make one each. When he returned to Messingham the new bells were ringing, but making the extraordinary sound of 'Ting, Tong, Pfuff'. They were made of tin, wood and leather!

Metheringham

Metheringham is a large village sitting comfortably between the Heath to the west and the Fens to the east. It has developed a large suburban sprawl so that to the south it almost reaches to Blankney, perhaps accounting for British Rail's confusion − the station is called 'Metheringham' but the signal-box is named 'Blankney'. Before the days of Beeching, the station combined the names of both villages.

Metheringham is famous for its World War II airfield, which is in the process of being converted into an interesting museum. Again names can be confusing, for the airfield is well out of Metheringham, much closer to Martin!

RAF Metheringham is most famous for the exploits of Norman Jackson. In April 1944 Jackson was a flight engineer on one of 106 Squadron's Lancaster bombers, returning home from a raid on Germany. They were attacked by a German fighter and one of the engines caught fire, resisting normal methods of extinguishing the flames.

Fearing that the wing-mounted petrol tanks would explode, Jackson decided to climb out onto the wing with an extinguisher in his hands. He put on a parachute and pulled the ripcord so that his friends inside the plane could hang onto the cords for him and so prevent him being blown off the wing. Using this precarious method, he was extinguishing the flames when the German fighter returned − wounding him in the back and legs.

Jackson lost his grip on the wing and was pulled round to the rear of the plane, fire beginning to singe the cords of his parachute. Fortunately his friends realised the danger, and let go of him; Jackson fell free, but on his descent his parachute cords proved to be on fire and he had to beat at the smouldering cords to prevent fire engulfing his parachute. For this incredibly brave attempt to save the lives of his colleagues, Jackson was awarded the Victoria Cross in October 1945, having spent much of the intervening period in hospital and prison camp.

The parish of Metheringham is enormous, but only in an east-west direction, where it extends from the river Witham to the A15. North to south it is squeezed between the equally elongated parishes of Blankney and Dunston. This curious pattern gave every village a share of the varied landscape of Heath down to Fen. At the very end of the parish, where the A15 crosses the B1202, can be found the remains of Metheringham Heath school. This is, in effect, a memorial to the depopulation of rural Lincolnshire, for the families of farm workers that once provided the school's pupils have gone, largely replaced by machinery.

Morton (Lindsey)

Morton is really a suburb of Gainsborough nowadays, but it grew up as a separate village on a difficult bend in the river Trent. Perhaps it has also been a rival to Gainsborough – so that there have been claims that Morton was the setting for George Eliot's *Mill on the Floss*, rather than the larger town nearby. Morton Hall is also said to have been where Eliot did most of the writing for this book.

Morton is also usually associated with the Danes. In 1013 Sweyn landed here and camped close to the village, perhaps causing the rumours that the earthworks towards Thonock to the east were a Danish camp, in fact they are those of a medieval castle. It was while staying in the area that Sweyn rudely ridiculed a monk who brought a message of warning from the long-dead Saint Edmund, but he became ill soon afterwards and said that he had been pierced by Edmund who thus took the considerable credit for Sweyn's eventual death. Sweyn's son, Cnut (or Canute) is also linked with the area, though he became a Christian and behaved more reasonably; some have claimed that the famous 'wet feet' incident involving Cnut took place in the river Trent and referred to the Aegir (*see Alkborough*) rather than the tide of the sea.

Moulton

The village is based upon the silt ridge that stretches east from Spalding to Holbeach, but the parish is enormous, stretching from the Wash almost to the county boundary, and it owes its size to fenland reclamation. The position of the hamlet of **Moulton Seas End** indicates where the sea once came.

Just north-east of the village, on one of the lanes leading off the main road, is the Elloe Stone. This used to mark the spot where, in medieval times, the wapentake met to hold the hundred court – a hundred being the equivalent then of a district council. The stone is no longer in its original site. There was also a castle here, but little remains and its site can only be conjectured.

In the 1300s places like Moulton and neighbouring Weston were rich agricultural communities and among the largest populated settlements in the county. Hence the church, which is one of several claiming to be 'Queen of the Fens', though it is probably the only one with three fonts.

The attractive green was a large pit until the 1800s; near it were the stocks and whipping post. The village is dominated by the eight-storey mill, the tallest in the country when built in 1822.

With fenland drainage, Moulton threw out 'daughter' settlements. One of these **Moulton Chapel**, has a church that was originally octagonal although a chancel was added later and rather spoils the effect.

Weston is most notable for the Wykeham chapel, close to the Welland. The prior of Spalding, who was lord of both Weston and Moulton, had a country house there which was built in 1311 and the chapel is all that remains.

118

Nettleham

➤ Nettleham is almost the definitive commuter village as it has grown so enormously since the 1960s, but it is a historic settlement with features of interest that are definitely worth a visit.

The most interesting curio in Nettleham can be found in the churchyard, on the left side of the path, immediately after crossing the beck at its southern side. This is the gravestone of Thomas Gardiner, a 19 year old post-boy who was murdered in 1732.

The sad story behind this starts with a wicked pair, Thomas and Isaac Hallam. In January 1732 they waylaid a Mr Wright

The sad memorial to a murdered postboy at Nettleham

from Rasen near Middle Rasen, and murdered him. Then they proceeded towards Lincoln and, the following night, murdered poor Gardiner in Nettleham South Field near a place called Bunker's Hill.

The two Hallams were soon caught and found guilty of murder. Isaac was hanged in irons at Nettleham Field in March 1732, Thomas fainted at the sight of this, but was himself taken away to be hanged near Middle Rasen.

The bishops of Lincoln had a manor house at Nettleham which was badly damaged in the 1536 revolt against Henry VIII's religious policies, and only earthworks now remain. Connected to it is a familiar-sounding legend that there was once an underground passage between Nettleham Manor and Lincoln Cathedral; apparently this can no longer be found – it had to be blocked up as sheep kept wandering into it. No doubt the sheep disrupted the sermon when they made their unexpected entrance! The manor dates from medieval times and was clearly once very important. It has been argued that Nettleham Methodist chapel stands on the site of the bishop's old private chapel. It has also been argued that Nettleham Manor was the place where in 1301 King Edward I declared his son to be the first Prince of Wales – not at Caernarfon at all.

Nettleham Hall (to the north-west and much nearer to Riseholme) was badly damaged by fire in the 1930s but is still worth a detour. The old gateway stands rather forlornly beside the road to Grange-de-Lings, itelf a monastic property that was an important gathering place during the Lincolnshire Rising of 1536. Of course this was inspired by some of Lincolnshire's monks, several of whom paid with their lives for their challenge to Henry VIII; no doubt this is the reason for Grange-de-Lings being supposedly haunted by the ghost of a headless monk.

Nettleton

➤ Nettleton sits in some quite dramatic scenery amidst the Wolds above Caistor. Like Caistor, it is associated with springs. Once of these, a 'tidal well' so it was said, was supposed to pour forth sand at regular intervals, thus accounting for the bed of sand in the area – and conveniently hindering periglacial activity. In 1695 the sand was referred to as having destroyed 25 houses in the previous 20 years, as well as a great hedge. Of course it may have been that sand-slips caused the damage, rather than sandy outbursts from the 'tidal well'.

Nettleton stands by an outcrop of iron in the Wolds. This has been quarried and even mined beneath Nettleton Top until 1969. The Viking Way, moving south out of Nettleton, actually uses a short tunnel that was part of the mining infrastructure.

Over a mile to the west of the village, at the foot of the Wolds and in the park of **Holton-le-Moor**, east of the house, was a 'wishing well' – another form of spring. This was famous for its medical cures and, when a tree grew there, it was soon festooned by superstitous visitors with pieces of cloth in honour of the spirits of the well. Holton Hall belonged to the Dixon family, one of whom designed the village hall in 1910. It is a strange building, rather unusually decorated with oddments relating to famous battles.

Nocton

➤ Nocton is dominated in history by its famous hall, though the present building was built only after the great fire of 1834 which destroyed its predecessor. From Norman times the Nocton estate belonged to the d'Arcy family, and it was Robert d'Arcy who founded Nocton Priory in about 1135. The remains of this can be found at **Wasp's Nest**, on the rising ground to the west of the Roman Car Dyke.

The d'Arcy family gave much land to the priory, but their relationship with the monks was not always a good one. In 1315 Philip d'Arcy accused the prior of employing cattle rustlers, and the prior retaliated by accusing d'Arcy of stealing the priory's farm implements.

Another highlight in the annals of Nocton was the visit of Henry VIII and Catherine Howard in 1541. The queen was persuaded to plant a chestnut tree near the house, and this is reputedly the one that still stands, though shored up with timber. The estate also belonged, briefly, to the tragic Lady Jane Grey.

Nocton Hall was rebuilt in the 1670s by Sir William Ellys who salvaged some materials from a manor house that had been built out of the old priory buildings. Ellys's efforts included a building known as The Pheasantry which may have been a banqueting hall. It was wrongly said to be a place where food was served to travellers in a tradition that lasted for 250 years. This building can still be seen, though Ellys's other efforts vanished in the fire.

Ellys's monument can be seen in the church, a notable Victorian effort by Sir George Gilbert Scott. The Ellys monument is now in its third home after a succession of church constructions in Nocton.

In the late 1700s the estate belonged to George Hobart, who married Albinia, the daughter of the Duke of Ancaster. Albinia was sadly addicted to gambling, and ruined the fortunes of the family. Another mistress of Nocton was Eleanor Eden, who jilted William Pitt, the famous politican, who never married anyone else. F.J. Robinson, another owner, was prime minister in the 1820s but was said to be 'as firm as a bullrush', though he enjoyed more success as chancellor of the exchequer.

This century the hall has been greatly used as a hospital, but visitors should also enjoy the village, which is notable for its estate buildings by Scott.

The hamlet of Wasp's Nest in the parish of Nocton, at the edge of the fen, is an interesting place to visit. The route of the Car Dyke can be traced and the site of the priory found though public access is limited. One can easily conceive that the monks at Leicester chose Nocton Priory as a place to send their problem colleagues! It is hard to imagine that this isolated spot was once the hub of an extensive narrow-gauge railway network built to serve the potato growing estates of Smith's Crisps who owned Nocton Hall itself for a time.

North Thoresby

The most interesting spot in North Thoresby, at least for those interested in local folklore, has always been the field immediately north of the church known as Bond Croft. In this field was a blue stone – a glacial erratic – where the manor court used to meet in medieval times after processing from **Autby**, which is itself now a deserted medieval village.

The stones in the area have legends attached which date back long before the Normans. At this time there was a prominent and muscular local citizen named Grim, who earned a living by fishing, thereby creating the momentum that eventually led to Grimsby becoming famous.

Grim heard that the king of the Danes had two magic stones. If these were each struck with branches of hazel, they would make the rain fall and the crops grow. Grim and his friend Boundel decided that these magic stones would be rather useful, so set off across the North Sea to purloin them.

Grim and Boundel, both big men, managed to sneak ashore at night and steal the stones, though they were very heavy. Once out at sea they discovered the foolishness of their enterprise, for the heavy stones were causing the boats to sink. Only by jettisoning everything else on board did they make it back to Lindsey.

They landed at Tetney and decided to send the stones to the king, but nobody else could lift them. Grim and Boundel began to stagger south with them, but the stones seemed to get heavier with each step. Crossing the Old Fleet at Grainsby bridge, the stones proved too much – timbers broke and Grim was thrown into the mud.

Boundel had gone on ahead and had crossed the bridge without problem. He had got as far as North Thoresby but then turned back to help, having left his stone in a field there. Neither of the stones could ever be moved again, but the locals put them to good use. Boundel's stone made rain and Grim's made the corn grow. Every year there was a 'whipping festival' to make the stones perform their tricks until, apparently, the Devil stole Grim's stone.

In later times a manorial court used to be held at Autby and a procession walked from there to Boundel's stone, carrying hazel wands. However over the centuries the field's name has altered from Boundel's Croft to Bond Croft.

Norton Disney

➤ Although it would no doubt boost the Lincolnshire tourist trade if there was a proven connection between Norton and the well-known Disney creations, the village's name derives from the Norman settlement of Isigne near Bayeaux. It became connected with the D'Isigny family after the Conquest, a name eventually anglicised as Disney.

A curiously unfortunate member of the family was Molineux Disney, who married in 1633 and had 13 children. Six of these were boys, but only one boy reached adulthood and he was hanged for felony! Perhaps because of all this misery the Disneys sold the lordship in 1674.

Old Bolingbroke

➤ Bolingbroke is an essential place to visit, if only because it is the one place in Lincolnshire where a king was born. Henry of Bolingbroke, born in 1367, was the son of John of Gaunt; both were key figures in the 14th century power struggle. Henry deposed Richard II in 1399 and claimed the throne as Henry IV, beginning the Lancastrian dynasty but causing much bloodshed in ensuing generations.

It is probable that the first fortification at Bolingbroke was on Dewy Hill to the north, but the castle had been constructed on the present site by 1232. This position was much lower and closer to the fenland, but the possibility of drainage problems was eased by digging a moat and using the spoil to raise the ground level within the wall. South of the castle was a 'rout yard' where stray cattle were collected, much like a pinfold in other villages, though this may have been originally intended to accommodate soldiers and their supplies in tents. The man who had the castle built was probably the Earl of

Chester, Randulph de Blundevill, who had fallen out with the king in about 1220.

De Blundevill had also been created the Earl of Lincoln in 1217 and this title passed to the de Lacy family, who spent much time at Bolingbroke and entertained Edward I there. Those were the halycon days, but by the 15th century the castle was in decline; one brief highlight being its use as a prison for Charles, Duke of Orleans.

A totally unedifying tale about the de Lacy family concerns the widowed Alice, Countess of Lincoln, who, in 1336, was kidnapped by Hugh de Frenes with the assistance of Sir John de Lacy. She was taken to Somerton Castle where she was raped. The king, Edward III ordered Frene's arrest but he escaped.

One story connected with Bolingbroke is that, during the 1536 Rising, the Chancellor of Lincoln was staying at the chantry priest's house as he was ill. There he was caught by rebels, who killed him though he promised them 20 shillings for his freedom.

Bolingbroke Castle became important again in the Civil War, starting as a Royalist stronghold (though semi-derelict). By October 1643 it was being challenged by Parliamentary forces and resisted a rather half-hearted siege for several days; however, the Royalists abandoned it after their side's defeat at Winceby. Parliament then had much of the castle pulled down to prevent further Royalist activity.

The village church was once much larger, due largely to investment by John of Gaunt. What is now the nave was once only the south aisle, but the church was badly damaged during the Civil War and left in a state of decay until Victorian times.

In 1776, Mary Longley, a suicide, was buried by the roadside near the old rectory, which faced the former green. To prevent her restless spirit from haunting the neighbourhood a stake was driven through her heart.

A Bolingbroke tradition was the 'pin and candle auction', though the idea was adapted from elsewhere. In 1938 John Ramsden gave some land to the parish and local people auctioned it off by means of a candle with a pin inserted about an inch from the top. Bidding continued until the candle flame reached the pin, which then dropped, signalling the end of the auction, and the last bidder became the owner of the land. There were conditions; no poultry was to be kept, and only two horses. Girl Guides were to be allowed to camp there at Whitsun.

Owston Ferry

➤ Owston Ferry was once an important place, for Kinnard Castle stood here to guard the passage of the river Trent and to control the ferry across it. The castle can best be located today by heading for the church, which stands within the earthworks of the castle bailey. The main earthworks can be seen to the south. It had a brief and inglorious history, being captured from the Mowbrays by Henry II in 1174. To complete the castle theme, the entrance to the churchyard from the east consists of an unusual triple arch; it looks like part of a castle's defences, but was built in 1859.

Until the 18th century there was a substantial house here instead of a castle. It was demolished in 1788 by Rev Robert Pindar who wanted to keep it away from a detested aunt; Pindar seems to have become prematurely aged and closed the house up before getting rid of it altogether.

Another Pindar is buried in the chancel of Owston church, with the unusual inscription 'This stone was laid down by S Smith'. This is thought to have been a Sally Smith, who had hoped to inherit the family's other property at Brumby from one of the Pindars and waited every day for the postman to bring the letter. Eventually she despaired and hanged herself from a bed post – the day the letter arrived. Her ghost used to haunt the park at Brumby near Scunthorpe.

Down the Trent from Owston Ferry is the hamlet of **Kelfield**. Strange events occurred here in about 1805. A man from West Butterwick named John Clarke went to West Stockwith fair but did not return home. At the time a brig was anchored at Kelfield, and its captain had a vivid dream of a man who was robbed and thrown in a river to drown. He saw the body float down the river and catch in the cable of a boat. When the captain awoke he rushed outside and found that his dream was true – Clarke's body was ensnared in the cable of his own brig. Two men were arrested but there was not enough evidence to prove the accusations against them.

Partney

➤ Partney is believed to have been a flourishing market town up until Norman times, after which it began to struggle in rivalry with Spilsby, where a new market was set up by the powerful Willoughby family. Long before the Normans, Partney had its own monastery, which was revived as a cell of Bardney in about 1115. By 1491 it was 'devastated', and much the same thing seems to have happened to Partney's role as a market town. The Partney sheep fair was eclipsed long before Horncastle's famous horse fair.

According to tradition, it was the plague that finally gave Spilsby the advantage. The very attractive house opposite the church on the Skegness road is know as the Plague House, so named because of the plaque that can be seen on its eastern gable: 'O Lord be thou my keeper, mercie and peace be in this place, 1616'. Sadly, even this interesting curiosity, though at present it can be viewed from a public footpath, seems to be disappearing beneath a creeper. Traditionally, the Plague House was the only one in Partney spared from the 1616 plague.

There was certainly still a market at Partney in the 1600s as the curate of Asgarby was also clerk of Partney market and additionally running an alehouse.

Matthew Flinders, the explorer, was married at Partney in 1801 and there is a memorial to this in the churchyard, which once possessed an oak said to have lived for 1,000 years. The church is also known for its weather-vane in the shape of a ship.

Potterhanworth

➤ The best-known legend about Potterhanworth involves a traveller who was lost on the Heath in the 1700s – presumably before Dunston Pillar was erected. Amidst a gathering storm and the darkening skies, the traveller was glad to hear the sound of a tolling bell and eventually saw a light. Thus guided into Potterhanworth, he found a warm welcome and a safe bed. He promised to repay the village for his deliverence, and bought a cottage and garden to be used as the home for the oldest poor man in the village on the condition that he rang the bell every winter night at seven o'clock.

A similar story has been told about a number of other Lincolnshire villages, as has another tale attached to the Potterhanworth curfew bell. This is that a young lad was told to guide his horse and cart across the Heath by keeping the bell on his right – as a result of which he made a complete circuit of the village and returned to his starting point! The bell was replaced by a clock in 1890.

The most prominent building in Potterhanworth is the Edwardian water tower. This was built after a long dispute over the village's traditional water supply ended with it being condemned by the medical officer of health. Even then the parish council refused to accede to the demands of progress, and held up work for four years.

Eventually a new bore hole was sunk and the tower built on the site of the old village pinfold. It was designed so that a room at the base of the tower could be used for parish functions and the original intention was that there should also be a 'garden of pleasure'.

Redbourne

➤ Redbourne once had a small castle, but this has disappeared apart from its earthworks to the south-west of the church. Perhaps it was once the scene of good living, for it is said that a man digging in the moat once found a silver cup. By tradition, the stone of the castle was used to build the church itself.

The church has one of the most interesting stained glass windows in Lincolnshire. Made in about 1840 by William Collins, it is based on a famous painting of 1826 by Francis Danby. The subject is the opening of the Sixth Seal in the Book of Revelation, with the consequent earthquake, the sun becoming as black as sackcloth and the moon turning the colour of blood. Danby is said to have been the beneficiary of Royal Academy politics for the Academicians turned up their noses at John Martin's similar paintings, though Martin has been seen as the inspiration of Danby and his artistic superior. Other features of interest in the church include several tombs of the St Albans family.

The 18th century smithy is notable for a leaping horse that adorns its gable.

Revesby

Revesby is famous for its abbey – both the actual one, long since demolished, and the stately home that has taken the name but is on a different site. The real Revesby Abbey was to the south of the village church and was founded in 1142 by William of Roumara. The founder became a monk himself in his old age and his tomb was uncovered during excavations of the site in 1869. Edward Stanhope, of the more modern Revesby Abbey, marked the site of the high altar with a stone slab, and various fragments of the building were placed in the parish church where they can still be seen.

Also in the church was a small 'building', possibly used as a reliquary in about the 14th century. It came from an earlier church on this site. In the churchyard is a gravestone from 1761, of a young man; it shows two hands, with one putting a ring upon the finger of another. The legend is that the young man was placing the ring on his bride's finger when he died of heart failure – certainly a sad tale.

After the dissolution of the abbey, the estate was developed. In 1714 it passed to the Banks family of London, and Joseph

Banks spent much time in the area as a result. He became a famous botanist and naturalist, linked forever with Botany Bay and voyages to Australia, and has been credited as the first Englishman to see a kangaroo – whether or not this is a significant accolade may be a matter of dispute. In 1778 he became President of the Royal Society, a more significant honour. The house was rebuilt in 1844.

Revesby also had a notable fair, at which the game of Single was popular. Six blindfolded 'hunters' had to catch a seventh man, who was festooned with bells. This man, the 'gingler', got a guinea if he evaded capture for a set period but lost the money if he used violence.

The Revesby 'barrows', which are beside the main road, have been claimed as prehistoric, but this seems unlikely. Another suggestion is that they were rabbit warrens, but this view does not seem entirely convincing either.

Rippingale and environs

➤ There are a large number of small villages between the 'dip' slope of the limestone and the Fen edge north of Bourne. Most of them had parishes of a very elongated shape, stretching for miles east into the fens.

In the 14th century Rippingale had a 'Jordon Cross', which was a wooden statue close to what is now the A15. Several miracles had occurred there and the result was a thriving trade in preaching, bell-ringing and processions. However, attempts by a local clergyman to have a chapel built there met with opposition; there was a lot of rivalry in the miracle trade at the time. However, a licence to build a chapel was granted by the Pope and it survived for about 200 years, latterly as a hermitage.

Rippingale church has a body brush, used to brush the feet of the dying to soothe them in about 1700. Buried in the churchyard, but unmarked, is Anne Hardy who died in 1815 aged 16 – she was 7 ft 2 ins tall!

Aslackby (Azelby) is known as a former preceptory of the Knights Templar. Substantial parts of this survived long after the Templars were suppressed – their round church stood until about 1800 and the gatehouse at Temple Farm was demolished as late as 1887. Now all that survives is a pinnacle in the garden of the farm – **Temple Bruer** has done better. **Dunsby** had a chalybeate spring near Hall Close, as does **Stainfield** still – close to the west edge of Dunsby Wood. These used to attract visitors. Stainfield once had its own 'chapel of ease' but it fell down in the 18th century. It also failed to develop as a spa as Dr Edward Greathead had intended in the 1720s and the well house was money sunk and lost.

Hacconby seems to vary in how many 'c's it has. Also confusing is the doubt over whether there was a small priory to the west of Hacconby church. This was certainly an accepted belief for many years, as was the view that parts of it had been used to build a farmhouse. There was a tradition that a stone reused in the farm had a hole in it, and the 'crier' for cattle would place a finger in there before calling them.

Riseholme

Riseholme is now an agricultural college which is the latest phase in a very varied history. The house, beautifully positioned on a lake, is one of the most attractive scenes in the Lincoln area and well worth a visit. There was once a village of Riseholme, and the earthworks of this can be seen near the lake opposite to the house. Its old church, on the west side of the site, had fallen into disrepair by the time of Elizabeth I and it seems that the village was virtually abandoned soon afterwards.

The house was built in the 18th century but then enlarged in 1840-5 when it was bought as a palace for the Bishop of Lincoln. Some extension was deemed necessary for this new use, and it is the Bishop's house that is largely the one we see today.

Ruckland, Farforth and Maidenwell

➤ Three tiny hamlets in the eastern Wolds; evidence of the continuous decline in the population of this area since medieval times.

Ruckland is said to have the smallest church in Lincolnshire, though even the word chapel would seem rather grand for this tiny building. The woods around Ruckland are said to be haunted by a 'shag boy', who may be related to the semi-naked 'wild man' seen in other parts of the county.

Farforth and **Maidenwell** were once on a route from Louth to Horncastle, but now they fit into a pattern of 'cul-de-sac' villages in the Wolds. A legend is told of a Farforth man who took to drink after the death of his wife, shutting himself up in one room and consuming alcohol continuously. Eventually hallucinations – or delirium tremens – began to affect him, and he dreamt that he was looking around Hell when he saw his wife in a magnificent armchair surrounded by devils. Nearby some other devils were making another armchair, which was clearly for his own use after death! One of the satanic workers left off his labours to tell the man that they were coming to get him as soon as the chair was finished. The man gave up drinking from that moment on, later going off to London to start afresh. However he died soon after and was brought back to Farforth for burial.

The name of the hamlet of Maidenwell indicates that it is sited at an old spring, one that was once actually enclosed by the old house here. Like some of the 'blow wells', it was said to rise and fall under the influence of the Trent. The actual village has long since declined and the church has been lost; for many years the area was turned over to a rabbit warren. It has been alleged that Bonnie Prince Charlie stayed here in the 1740s while making a trip from Saltfleetby (where he landed in a French ship) to Lincoln. This story seems to have been an attempt to blacken the name of Mr Moseley, a Catholic landowner; after he died in 1745 his coffin was exhumed to check that he had not 'staged' his own death in order to run off to France to join the Young Pretender.

Ruskington

━ Nowadays Ruskington's reputation seems to be mostly related to food. Its chip shop, the 'Elite', has won the title for the best fish and chips in the country, while the butcher in the High Street has also been 'Lincolnshire Sausage Champion'. In the past its reputation was more to do with drink; in the mid-1800s the situation was so bad that there would be three of four different fights going on in the High Street at one time. Life was said to be so exciting that sometimes the carrier's waggon from Dorrington to Sleaford never got to its destination, the driver preferring to stop in Ruskington to watch the battles!

All this changed when a temperance campaign began in 1857, transforming the character of the village. A stone slab in the modernised newspaper shop shows a link with those times, and in Jubilee Street can be seen the teetotal almshouses that were put up for elderly non-alcoholics. These, built in 1887, are interesting examples of late-Victorian architecture.

Along the road to Lincoln is an important Anglo-Saxon burial site. In 1871 during gravel excavations two skeletons were found, one placed above the other. In 1936 a further four skeletons were discovered. When the bungalows were being built to the north of the old windmill in 1942-5, further graves were found in the ditch at the front of the houses and in a gravel pit just to the west. This area partly overlies the course of a Roman road.

Saltfleet

━ An unusual and interesting village with much to absorb the visitor. Saltfleet is really a part of the parish of Skidbrooke, or that is how it began. Skidbrooke is a mile inland, but it has declined inexorably and the church is now quite remarkably isolated in the loneliest of fields.

Saltfleet itself began life as a fishing haven in medieval times, developed a market as well (which failed) and in the late 1700s found a new popularity as a bathing place. However it is a curious feature of Saltfleet that one can stand in the middle of the village and have virtually no idea that it is on the coast at all.

Saltfleet once had a church, but rather like Mablethorpe's St Peter's church, it disappeared into the sea years ago. In 1821 fishermen at Saltfleet caught the clapper of a large bell in their nets, and this was said to be from Saltfleet's old church, but it was more likely to have been from a ship's bell as there have been many wrecks in the area. For example, in 1894 the *Olive Branch* and the *Annie Florence* sank on the same night; six drowned from the former, while seven men survived by clinging to an upright mast. In 1880 another relic dragged from the sea was a pewter flagon; this was also said to be from the church.

In the middle of Saltfleet, at right angles to the road, is the manor house. Cromwell is said to have spent a night there in 1643, and the house is also reputed to be haunted by a beautiful lady who would sit on a windowsill during daylight hours. Another rumoured visitor to Saltfleet is said to have been Bonnie Prince Charlie, who landed at Saltfleet in 1744 on a scouting mission. It is said that he stayed overnight at Maidenwell, then went to a masked ball in Lincoln; quite why he needed to spy out Lincolnshire is unexplained.

The New Inn originated in the 1600s and was extended in the 1700s, probably to accommodate the bathing trade. Even this building has rumours attached, saying that it was first built on the beach but was moved inland wholesale in 1862. Sadly, this story is nonsense too! It seems more likely that there was a more temporary hotel on the beach at some stage in the early 1800s when Saltfleet was at its most popular as a resort. It was also rather notorious then, being described as 'Little Sodom' by a clergyman.

More in the realms of proven historical fact is the village pump, which was erected as a memorial to Frederick Freshney, a trooper in the Boer War who was wounded in battle in 1899, came back to Saltfleet, and died there of his wounds six years later. While in South Africa he was involved with rescuing an armoured train which had been attacked by the Boers, during which a certain Winston Churchill had been captured. In his memoirs Freshney described the train '. . . coming slowly with its load of dead and wounded. The poor wounded fellows were lying on the coals, some on the cow-catcher, some on top of the boiler, and one even clinging to the chimney.'

The marsh on the south side of Saltfleet is said to be haunted by the ghost of a man who broke his neck while riding horseback across the area.

The saddest place in Saltfleet is the garden of the Methodist chapel, which has been designed as peaceful but sad memorial to the people of Saltfleet who lost their lives in the flood of 1953 when the sea poured through Sea Lane, trapping several elderly people in bungalows.

Saltfleetby parishes

➤ Three scattered and lonely villages, seeming to lack even a discernible centre, but united in having some curious events in their church history. The traditional pronunciation is 'Sollerby'.

Saltfleetby St Clement's is no longer a church at all, but a craft and tea shop. It was built in about 1225 a quarter of a mile from the main road, but by Victorian times this arrangement had become rather inconvenient. In 1885-6 the rector had the church taken down piece by piece, each stone numbered, and then rebuilt beside the road – apparently to avoid a tramp across muddy fields.

Saltfleetby St Peter has an old and new church, of which the old is much the most interesting. It is a romantically ruined tower, surrounded by trees and seemingly enveloped by nature since being abandoned. It is a beautiful spot and so it is easy to understand the well-wisher who left money to maintain this ruin. Only the tower remains, the rest of the church having been demolished. Much of the old church was reused in the new one, on the main road, and it is believed that the new church largely copied the plan of the old.

Close to the old church is a 'prospect tower', a viewpoint erected as a folly in about 1812.

The church at Saxby

Saxby

Saxby is notable for its Georgian church, which was originally built as a private mortuary chapel for the Earls of Scarborough. The sixth, seventh and eighth Earls have memorials inside.

The first Earl of Scarborough came from the Saunderson family, but the title passed to Viscount Lumley in 1690 – hence Lumley Road in Skegness. Earlier in the 1600s the Lumleys had been wealthy but had no title, at which time John Lumley was an aging man with no heir. As he was riding near Loughborough he heard a boy called out by his surname 'Lumley', and chose the boy to be his heir. This boy became the first Viscount Lumley in 1628.

Saxby church is unusual in not having a proper belfry, and the bell-rope dangles immodestly in the portico. Perhaps this was a convenience in days gone by, when the church bell was used to proclaim fire or catastrophe. It was abused on at least one occasion, when a local knave tied a donkey's tail to the bell – causing all to rush around in fear of fire!

A mile north of Saxby is **Normanby-by-Spital**, traditionally pronounced 'Norramby'. A mile to the east of here is Gibbet Post Farm, where a tree was apparently used as a gibbet. The irons were later used for the foundations of a bridge.

Saxilby

Saxilby is best known for its position of the Fosse Dyke, the canal cut by the Romans to connect the Witham to the Trent and one of the foundations of Lincoln's fortune. However, Saxilby is also infamous for its connection with the notorious murderer, Tom Otter, who bludgeoned his new wife to death in 1805 and was later gibbeted beside the lane from Broadholme to Thorney.

Otter was a young man who was rather too free with his sexual favours, as a result of which a young girl found herself pregnant. Otter was pressed into marrying her, but took the first opportunity to murder her with a hedge stake. The dead woman was soon discovered and her corpse taken to the Sun Inn at Saxilby where it was first placed on the mounting stone outside and then on a table with the hedge stake nearby. Otter was arrested in the room beside the mounting stone when the sun, shining through the window, showed up the bloodstains on his shirt.

When Otter was gibbeted he became the source of much local interest, especially after a bird's nest was discovered in his skull. When the gibbet rotted and fell down, it was turned into souvenirs by a Lincoln entrepreneur. The hedge stake proved tougher, though, for although it became a pub curio it developed a frightening tendency to return to places connected with its grim history. It was pinned to a wall at a pub at Torksey Lock, but on the anniversary of the murder was mysteriously ripped from its position. Then it was stapled to the wall of the Peewit Inn by a local blacksmith, but again it was ripped away, and the staples thrown through the blacksmith's window. In the end the Bishop of Lincoln ordered that the hedge stake be burnt in Minster Yard.

One of the most curious features of the Tom Otter story is that, years afterwards, a man named John Dunkerley confessed that he had witnessed the murder. He was half drunk at the time, having been at the Sun Inn, and did not tell anyone until he was dying.

Scawby

━ Scawby is an interesting area, reached rather suddenly after the drab industrial wasteland of eastern Scunthorpe. In the woods to the west of the village are the famous 'Gull ponds' which developed into a spectacular breeding site for seagulls after the draining of nearby lands in the 1830s and 1840s. Apparently the ponds became infested with eels and this attracted the gulls, which came in large numbers from about 1842. Access to the ponds is possible by various paths from the nearby motorway bridge.

Scawby Hall dates from the early 1600s and was the home

of the Nelthorpe family. Richard Nelthorpe was executed in London in 1685 for his role in the Duke of Monmouth's rebellion against James II. Later Nelthorpes were early patrons of George Stubbs, who spent several years at Horkstow. Demolished in 1977 to make way for the motorway was an unusual 'Roman Bridge' in Scawby Park; it was probably 18th century, but seems to have been a largely decorative feature that doubled up as a boathouse.

More easy to see is the Victorian mansion of Scawby Grove, built out of one of the first Scunthorpe 'iron' fortunes and as showy as one would expect. It belonged to the Cliff family, who came from Yorkshire but established a successful business at Frodingham.

Station Farm, south of the village, is a rare example of an inn being built for the railway but later converted into a farm.

Just north of the A18 is one of several 'lost' villages in the district – **Raventhorpe**.

Scotter

➤ According to tradition, Scotter was the manor of Brand, an uncle of Hereward the Wake, and subsequently Abbot of Peterborough to which he presented the manor. It is certainly a place with a long history, for a boat fashioned from a tree trunk was once found near the river Eau and this was believed to date from before the Norman Conquest. The name of the river is also worthy of mention since the Ordnance Survey labels it as the 'Eau' whereas some earlier sources call it the 'Eea' or 'Ea' – being old English for river.

Half a mile west of the village, on the east bank of the West Beck, is some land once known as The Bellbutts. This dates from the time Henry VIII banned all sports and decreed that males aged 16 to 60 should practise archery on parish land. In fact by the 1700s the land had found other parish uses, being the place where local youths went after church on a Sunday for wrestling and football matches.

Near the river stands the Old Manor House. A curiosity of this is a plaque claiming that one wing was built in the year 5710, a date reached by calculating the age of the earth according to the misguided Dr Usher, the Irish prelate whose *Annales Veteris et Novi Testamenti* (1650-4) claimed on scriptural grounds that the date of the creation was 4004 BC.

King John stayed at the manor house in 1216 while his men were lodged at a nearby inn. The landlord was delighted and adopted the arms of the officer in charge – the Sun and Anchor.

Scrivelsby

➤ Scrivelsby is famous as the home of the hereditary 'Champions of England', the Marmion and Dymoke families. It was the job of the Champion to appear at every coronation, mounted on a white horse, and to challenge to battle anyone who would dispute the monarch's title to the crown. From the time of Richard II for years this was the task of the Marmions, but then it passed to the Dymokes through marriage and Sir John Dymoke was the Champion at the crowning of Lincolnshire's only king, Henry of Bolingbroke – perhaps a rather risky task, under the doubtful circumstances!

The Champion usually made a dramatic entrance during the coronation feast, throwing down a gauntlet and declaring his readiness to fight. After no one had accepted the challenge, the Champion was awarded a special cup and the right to the armour he wore as a fee. The last time the gauntlet was thrown down was at the coronation of George IV in 1821, after which the Champion carried a standard instead. It is a sad comment on the decline of a landed family that the Dymokes were later forced to sell the coronation cups. The decline of the family was also speeded by complex inheritances and two disastrous fires. This led to the 'Champion of England' being imprisoned for debt in Dublin in 1868, but he also complicated the affairs of the estate by having a son by the girl (she was only 15 or 16) who became his wife 13 years later, but who was never fully acknowledged. This son, Gilmore Dymoke, was nonetheless buried in the churchyard at Scrivelsby.

The house was in ruins by 1938 and barely habitable. It was

finally demolished in 1956 though the gatehouse continues in use by the Dymokes. Access to the garden is sometimes possible. Visible from the main road, though, is the famous Lion Gateway of about 1833.

The church contains the tombs of some of the family and one monument has the strange symbol of a snake biting its own tail – a sign of eternity. When the church was being restored in the 19th century, the tomb of a man was found beneath the floor; strangely, he had no head, just a lump of clay. Once disturbed, his body crumbled to dust, leaving just the lump of clay. The body was believed to be that of Sir Thomas Dymoke, beheaded in 1470 for his part in a rebellion during the Wars of the Roses.

Scunthorpe

The town of Scunthorpe is a creation of the Victorian iron industry. Its rapid growth led to Scunthorpe officially becoming a town in 1919, when it was created out of **Appleby, Frodingham, Brumby, Crosby** and **Ashby**. Its growth means that it has now joined on to technically separate settlements like **Bottesford**.

The development of the iron industry really began in 1856 when Rowland Winn of Appleby Hall had some of the local stone analysed. The working of ore started in 1860 and construction of the first ironworks in 1863.

Scunthorpe is surrounded by a number of 'lost' villages. There is a particular concentration at **High** and **Low Risby** and **Sawcliffe**, just off the A1077. This includes a lost church, which may have helped to give rise to the 'sunken church' of Dragonby.

Dragonby was once called Conesby Cliff, but its name was changed by Gervase Elwes, a successful tenor singer, to take account of the strange rock formation just to the north of the village street, caused by a spring bubbling up through the limestone. This looks rather like the back of a half-buried dragon which apparently stopped to drink from the spring and was turned to stone by a wizard. It has also been claimed that it is a buried church that sank into the ground with all the congregation still inside; on the anniversary of the disaster, the bells can be heard ringing.

One of the greatest curiosities of Scunthorpe, though it is now not much more than a damp spot within a housing estate, is the Templar's Bath in Bottesford. This seems to have been an ancient spring roofed over with stone, into which one could descend by a few steps. As the Knights Templar once owned land at Bottesford, it seems to have become connected with them. It has also been suggested that it was a Roman hypocaust, but there are a number of other springs in the district. The Templar's Bath filled with mud about 100 years

The spring at Bottesford

ago, but quite close by is St John's Well – encased in a small Victorian structure.

Ashby possessed the last operative duck decoy in the county. This was still in use when the Friskney one was abandoned in 1878. The decoy was capable of capturing hundreds of birds at a time.

The Trent is crossed by the Keadby bridge, just south of which is **Althorpe**. There was a consternation here when the first steamboat was trialled on the Trent on a Sunday morning; according to a rather unreliable tradition. The congregation were all listening to a sermon about damnation when they were disturbed by what sounded like the puffing and roaring of a monster outside. They all rushed out in mortal fear – to see a steamboat passing by.

Within the town itself one has to look hard to find items of curiosity. Frodingham Hall, for example, has left us only a pair of gate pillars near the museum. The main survival, though hardly 'hidden', is Brumby Hall, a fine 17th and 18th century house. There has been a house here since at least the 14th century, but for several years this century it belonged to British Steel.

Sedgebrook

➤ Sedgebrook is one of several small villages just to the west of Grantham and in the shadow of Belvoir Castle, which is actually in Leicestershire. It is central to an interesting piece of the Lincolnshire landscape.

Newbo Abbey was founded here in 1198, south-east of the church. The abbey seems to have taken advantage of one of the common Lincolnshire wills which left land to finance the ringing of church bells at dusk. The abbey appointed a deacon whose sole job was to ring the bell both morning and evening each day except Sunday. Thus the monks could then appropriate the revenues from the land, which became known as deacon's glebe.

The village to the north, **Allington**, is really an amalgamation of East and West Allington. East Allington was a separate parish with its own church, but this was demolished in 1953.

143

There are several 'holy wells' in the area. On the minor road south of Allington there is a chalybeate spring called the Salt Well while the holy well at **Woolsthorpe-by-Belvoir** supplied the water for Belvoir Castle. However, it does not seem to have any power to protect the village from misfortune, for Woolsthorpe was occupied by the Parliamentary Army during the Civil War and its church burnt down. This church was south of the village, and left unrepaired; its tower fell down in about 1868 but the old graveyard can still be seen. The villagers used St Mary's chapel until 1791, when it was rebuilt as a proper church though the tower remained incomplete for the next century.

The pretty village of **Denton** also has a holy well named after St Christopher, in the woods beside one of the ponds. Here is a rare example of a holy well having been made into something, for it has been transformed into a grotto with a romantic verse about nymphs. The manor has been demolished.

Sempringham

A very important settlement in the history of Lincolnshire, yet it has vanished so completely (apart from its church) that it is not even named on the current 1:50,000 OS maps. In fact Sempringham consists of a lonely church between Billingborough and Pointon.

In 1083 Gilbert of Sempringham was born here, the son of the lord of the manor. Traditionally, it is said that before he was born his mother dreamt of holding a man in her lap; this was seen as a sign that her son would rise to greatness, but he was found to be deformed. Though hampered by deformity, he was clever and rapidly became respected within religious circles. He returned to Sempringham as its priest and founded a monastery there, which was unusual in that it was open to men and women. In 1148 he got a licence from the Pope for his monastery and the 'Gilbertine' order was founded.

By the time Gilbert died in 1189 (making him a reputed 106), there were twelve Gilbertine houses, many of them in

Lincolnshire. Their importance was further enhanced when Gilbert was declared to be a saint, following which the monastery at Sempringham was rebuilt on a massive scale. A central wall divided the male and female parts, into which was set Gilbert's shrine so that both sexes had access to it. A number of miracles led to Gilbert being declared a saint; one of these occurred while he was staying in London. A great fire had broken out in the neighbourhood; instead of running away, Gilbert remained at prayer and the fire passed around his house.

The priory did not always maintain Gilbert's high standards. In the late 1280s Edward I used it to imprison eight Welsh princesses, the daughters of Llewellyn, who had been killed in 1282. In the 14th century a notorious gang of robbers, the Folville brothers, were given shelter in the priory by Alan of Baston and also in one of the priory's granges – possibly the one to the east that was built over Car Dyke. Alan of Baston later paid the gang to destroy a rival's watermill.

Until 1938-9 it was assumed that the parish church had been the nave of the monastery. Major excavations, though, showed that the monastery had been a quarter of a mile to the south-west and had vanished totally after the dissolution. A mansion for Lord Clinton had been built with some of the materials. Also vanished is the village of Sempringham, which probably declined when the monastery developed; it was north-west of the church. One of the external features which can still be seen is the holy well, a natural spring that is credited with special powers.

Skegness

Perhaps Skegness cannot really qualify for a place in 'Hidden Lincolnshire' as it is probably the best known town in the county; in some ways, better known even than Lincoln itself.

The origins of the town are lost but we can be certain that the coastline around here has been constantly changing over the centuries. The Romans had a Saxon shore fort in the area, but that has gone, and the medieval town had largely disappeared into the sea by Tudor times in 1540. All of which leaves the old St Clement's church as something of a mystery, still a mile inland and now surrounded entirely by suburbia.

The rest of the town owes its existence to the seaside trade, which was established here by the 1770s, and developed by the Earls of Scarborough from 1878. The Earls had a house in Skegness, Old Hall, on the 'Roman' bank in the 1720s, but the place was unimpressive; John Byng visited in 1776 and found it 'this vile, shabby bathing place'. The earliest memento of the growth of Skegness is thus really the Vine Hotel in Vine Road, worth visiting as a rare example in the town of something from the 1700s; it was built about 1750, apparently close to where the seashore then was.

This century the town has been most closely associated with Billy Butlin, who began his local interest in 1926. From the same period and in a similar category of bizarre castellated follies as the silo at Ulceby, is the 'Sun Castle' along the seafront; probably the last 'Castle' built in Lincolnshire.

South of the town is the Gibraltar Point nature reserve, for decades a popular spot for outings. The area was declared a nature reserve in 1949 and the visitors' centre opened by David Attenborough in 1974. A boat turned upside down served as a family home there for many years, with 16 children being born in its two rooms.

Sleaford

➤ Sleaford today is a struggling market town, rather squeezed between the triangle of Boston, Grantham and Lincoln, and until 1993 suffering inordinately from excessive traffic. Now that relief from this has come, there is a chance that the town may develop more character and show its features of interest more clearly.

There are – or were – two Sleafords. Old Sleaford was on the line of the Roman road that now forms Mareham Lane, a delightful route that provides a rare opportunity for peaceful and relaxing driving. Old Place, on Boston Road, is one of the few reminders of Old Sleaford and belonged to Lord John Hussey, beheaded for his supine performance in the Rising of 1536 (*see Boston*). New Sleaford grew up as a planted town under the influence of the Bishop of Lincoln, Alexander, who built the castle between 1123 and 1139. Sleaford Castle falls well within the subject of 'Hidden Lincolnshire', for it is little known as there is but one fragment of wall remaining, held up rather inelegantly by a block of concrete.

Sleaford Castle is famous as the last stopping place of King John on his final journey to Newark, where he died. It is usually claimed that he died of poison administered to him by the monks of Swineshead Abbey, but it has also been suggested that he was killed by the new cider and peaches that he consumed during his stay at Sleaford.

The bishops of Lincoln maintained their interest in the castle and Sleaford as a useful source of revenue. In the 1430s and 1440s the bishops improved the link to Lincoln by building 'Broad Street', most of the present A15, and often also taken as being a Roman road.

The castle was in ruins by the 1600s and being used as a convenient quarry in the 1700s; two inns were said to be built from its stone.

Visitors should also go to the Market Square, which is dominated by St Denys' church, behind which to the north is one of the oldest vicarages in the country still in use, with parts of it dating back to 1568. The Bristol Arcade to the south was once a fine coaching inn.

The churchyard is worth inspection. In it there is an old window from the church, taken out during restoration in 1884, and also the old parish lock-up which was positioned unusually close to the church.

In a builders' yard just off Carre Street can be seen the very fine but rather decaying offices of the Slea Navigation, which was built in 1792-4. Navigation House was built in 1838 and deserves to be put to some better use – perhaps the revival of the Navigation will be its saving. Just beyond it can be seen the stone entrance to 'Navigation Wharf'. Further downriver is Cogglesford Mill, recently restored, and the scene of milling for centuries.

Southgate has effectively become Sleaford High Street since the opening of the railway. It has two historic pub signs; the Black Bull has a sign of 1689, which shows bull-baiting, but the building is much newer though the sign is claimed as the oldest pub sign 'in position' in the country. The White Hart has a stone sign of 1691, but alert visitors will notice that it does not quite match the hotel on which it is fixed!

In Northgate is a strange pair of cottages, Nos. 51 and 53. Built in 1749, they include a genuine Norman archway which could have come from either the castle or the church of Old Sleaford. Another old gate known to have come to Sleaford was from 'John of Gaunt's Palace' in Lincoln. It was put up at the manor house and in 1934 moved to Old Place. Sleaford seems to have been a collecting house for medieval fragments over the years, as there are others at Westholme.

Snitterby

➤ Snitterby is a small village with a bland Victorian church, but its previous church was rather more exciting. Only built in the 1700s the local congregation clearly lacked the ability to look after it, for by the mid-1800s it was in a terrible state. The font doubled up as a pudding basin (or the other way around), the altar was a three-legged table, the church often flooded and there was a hole in the chancel. Doubtless the latter was the cause of death of a Victorian parson, who expired from the draught, inspiring one of his successors to get a new church built.

Somersby and Tennyson Country

➤ Somersby will always be famous as the birthplace of Alfred Tennyson, the great Victorian poet. The son of an Anglican clergyman, he was born at what is now Somersby House in 1809 (but visitors often assume he was born in Somersby Grange, near the church) and spent his formative years roaming around the local countryside. The result is that every nook and cranny for miles around claims some form of Tennyson association. In the church itself is a collection of

Tennysoniana and outside is the grave of his father.

Especially imbued with Tennysonian associations is the Holywell Glen, a narrow valley through which the river Lymn runs to the north-west of Somersby. The Blackhill spring adds its waters to the Lymm and may be connected with the 'holy well' of the name, though it has also been said that there was once an actual well in the valley which was filled in after a child had an accident there. A sandstone bath-house in the Glen was later turned into a school, surely a delightful first school for Alfred. There was also a barber's shop here. All of this was, apparently, once 'a miniature Derbyshire', and it is claimed that Tennyson wrote *Maud* there, though this is also associated with Harrington Hall nearby.

Stockwith Mill, near Harrington, is said to be the inspiration behind Tennyson's *The Miller's Daughter*, once claimed as the poem which caught the attention of Victoria and Albert; in reality this was *In Memoriam*.

Less than a mile east of Somersby is **Bag Enderby**, which one suspects of having inspired Tolkien. Here was the 'Poet's Tree', which was planted by a rector and stretched across the Harrington road. To complete the arborial theme, elm trees once grew on the roof of the church here. On the front door of the church is a boss, supposed to have been from a Saxon shield.

In the parish of **Harrington** is, of course, Harrington Hall, now rebuilt after a disastrous fire. Its Tudor walled garden was said to be the inspiration for Tennyson's poem, *Come into the garden, Maud*.

Within the curiously shaped parish of Somersby now lies **Ashby Puerorum** and Holbeck Manor. Between the two lie Clapgate Lodge and Clapgate Farm, names that are connected with the battle of Winceby – but as usual there are two versions of the tale! One is that troops were camping on Hoe Hill before the battle, but could not sleep as a gate was clanging all night; it has been suggested that this was done deliberately to keep them awake. It has also been said that the gate 'clapped' a lot after the battle as the Royalists ran through it! Ashby Puerorum got its name as the ecclesiastical living was used to provide funds for the choirboys of Lincoln.

Holbeck Manor was built in 1823 and is notable for its

romantically landscaped grounds which can be seen from Hoe Hill, one of the best viewpoints in Lincolnshire. During the depression years between the wars, the owner of Holbeck Manor employed local people to construct a number of follies in the grounds. Some remains of these are still there, but the statues with which he decorated the gardens have gone.

Somerton

A castle built for the Bishop of Durham in the 13th century, in the 'summer pastures' alongside the Brant, which were often too wet for much use during the rest of the year.

There have been some interesting events in the castle over the years and it is, of course, reputed to be haunted. In 1336 Hugh de Frenes kidnapped Alice, the widowed Countess of Lincoln, from Bolingbroke Castle and took her to Somerton where she was raped. Sir Hugh was arrested on the king's orders but escaped.

In 1359 the castle was used to imprison King John I of France. Sadly for him, the stock of wine was vandalised just before his arrival. Four years later the castle was visited by Edward III but seems to have declined soon afterwards – it was falling down 30 years later.

The castle is not open to the public and is rather difficult even to see as it is surrounded by trees. The minor road follows the curve of the outer defences.

South Ferriby

South Ferriby is dominated by its cement works, fed with chalk from the Wolds a mile to the east. However its history is dominated by Ferriby sluice, a crucial link in the scheme to improve the river Ancholme and drain the Carrs in the 17th century.

When the sluice was being built in the 1630s there was a shortage of good building stone. A lot of it was taken from an old chapel of ease at West Butterwick on the Trent, and this is said to have brought a curse down upon the whole Ancholme scheme. One suspects that this story was a convenient ruse by opponents of drainage to explain mysterious accidents to the drainage works and to the Dutch labourers; labourers who disappeared without explanation were said to have been carried off by the 'Tiddy' folk, fairy-like creatures rumoured to be displeased about the destruction of their marshy habitat.

By 1724 the sluice was in a bad state and could not even be crossed on foot. Instead you had to trust yourself to 'a paltry short boat, commanded by a little old deaf fellow with a long beard'. William Stukeley, the 'Archdruid' antiquarian, described the ruined structure as 'like the picture of Hell gates in Milton'. It was all rebuilt in the 1760s – hopefully without any ecclesiastical remnants this time!

South Ferriby itself nestles in the lee of the Wolds scarp slope, though at this point the high ground is barely 200 feet. Springs attracted settlement, and one can still be seen gushing out water close to the main road. The site has been settled for a long time – Roman remains have been found here. The village church partly collapsed in 1492; apparently 'the sides flew out'.

To the north of Ferriby sluice can be seen Read's Island. This was much smaller in the early 1800s when it was known as Old Warp, and in the 1840s it was leased by a man named Read. He used it to fatten animals and employed a herdsman to live there in a hut – it must have been a lonely life. Queen Victoria had been dead for three months before one denizen of Read's Island knew about it. Apparently Sir John Rennie, the Scottish civil engineer, had a scheme in the early 1800s to connect the island to the mainland.

South Kyme

➤ South Kyme is a genuine surprise, so it is best to approach it from the direction that gives the most benefit – the north. Do not, however, tarry in **North Kyme**, which is a straggling

151

The remains of the 'tower house'

linear village strung out along the main road.

The village of South Kyme is heralded by a lovely vignette: the lonely church, with only an imposing tower and a beautiful hall for company. In fact the tower is what was left after a 14th century 'tower house' was partially demolished in the 1720s, and it is rarely if ever open for public access. During some of the 16th century it had belonged to Baron Tailboys of Kyme, who may have been able to gain his title as he did Henry VIII a favour by marrying one of the king's old mistresses – and the mother of Henry's illegitimate son.

The south face of the church (nearest to the lane) contains all that remains on the surface of the Augustinian priory that was once here, though the hummocks in the grassy field beyond the church to the north, show where other buildings once stood. Not surprisingly, the land there has been known as Abbey Yard for centuries. The lands passed to Sir Robert Tyrwhitt in 1541. Over the porch of the church can be seen some headless statues, once a fine carving of the Coronation of the Virgin.

The old Kyme family has many links with the history of

Lincolnshire, but one of the most intriguing concerns the arranged marriage of John Kyme with Ann Ayscough in the turbulent Tudor era. Ann's opposition to 'Popery' so annoyed her husband that he drove her out of his house at Kelsey. There is a sad end to the tale; Ann was burnt at the stake in Smithfield, London, in 1546.

South Ormsby

One of the many tiny villages in the eastern Wolds where depopulation has been a problem for a long time. This may explain why the area became the focus of one of the Diocese of Lincoln's first experiments at a 'group' of parishes. **Calceby**, a mile to the east, is a good example of a deserted medieval village with a romantically ruined church, in its time one of the best in the county. Part of the church was to be reused at South Ormsby.

South Ormsby stands at the beginning of one of the most beautiful roads in Lincolnshire – the prehistoric Bluestone Heath Road that runs along the edge of the Wolds to Caistor. This 'ridgeway' was later used by the Romans, who built a camp along it but it was ploughed up in about 1800.

The 'house' here was the second home for the Massingberds, better known for Gunby Hall. A rector here was Samuel Wesley, the rather irritable father of John and Charles. He had to resign the living after a quarrel in which he refused to meet a gentleman's mistress on a social basis; the gentleman was probably the Earl of Castleton, who rented the house for a while, though he may have been the Marquis of Normanby. However, Wesley moved on to Epworth and so the tourists visit there rather than South Ormsby. It seems unlikely that Wesley was sad to leave, as he described his time there in:

'. . . a mean cot composed of reeds and clay
Wasting in sighs the uncomfortable day.'

However, the Old Rectory is not the one that Wesley lived in. In later years the church living of South Ormsby tended to be given to a younger son of the Massingberds so that the family were in charge of both the bodies and the souls of local labourers.

Spalding

➤ Spalding is a town that owed its initial prosperity to its position on the river Welland, the positioning of a castle and a rich Benedictine priory – the latter being founded in 1087.

What there is to see of the old priory is debatable. The 'Prior's Oven', at the corner of Sheepmarket, is said by some to be the old priory prison dating from about 1320. It once had a bell which tolled during executions. It is said that when an execution was held, the bailiff of Pinchbeck provided the rope, that of Spalding led the prisoner to the gallows, the one from Weston carried the ladder, and the Moulton bailiff hanged the criminal. Later the Prior's Oven (also once known as The Turret) became a forge and a restaurant. On the theme of punishment, the town pillory used to be kept on four wheels so that it could be rolled out into the Market Place; its last 'inhabitant' was a woman in 1787, for keeping a house of ill repute.

Abbey Buildings in Priory Road are certainly contemporary with the existence of the priory, but the claim that they are the monks' dormitory seems unconvincing.

Relations between the monks and the townspeople, as in many other places, were not always good. When a parish church was first built, the monks only allowed it to have two bells, which were not to be rung when the monks were in bed; when the townspeople added three more, the prior complained to the king.

In the churchyard is the grave of William Lee, who was killed in a duel at the White Hart in 1723. While in the churchyard, take a look at the church steeple. A weather-cock was placed there in 1782 by William Cross; that night he celebrated his brave deed by getting drunk at the Bull Inn, after which he fell in the river Welland and drowned.

154

In 1710 the Spalding Gentlemen's Society was formed. This was a society for 'antiquaries' and included such notable members as William Stukeley and Isaac Newton. Its building can now be found in Broad Street. The Society was formed by Maurice Johnson, who had 26 children all by one wife; 16 of them sat down at the table together.

In 1714 Spalding was badly damaged by a fire which destroyed 84 buildings. A soldier who tried to create a fire-break using gunpowder blew himself up.

Ayscoughfee Hall is said to originate from about 1429, but has been altered many times since. The visitor will find much of general interest there as it houses the museum.

Spilsby

Spilsby is an interesting market town that has maintained a unique identity because it is not big enough to attract the faceless chain stores that have destroyed so many larger towns. It is a town made famous by its connections with two families – the Willoughbys and the Franklins.

The Willoughbys lived at **Eresby**, just south-west of the town, but their house was burnt down in 1769. All that remains in situ is a tall gate pillar surmounted by an urn. The site was first developed by the de Bek family, who gained a licence to crenellate their house there in 1276. The male line died out and the property passed by marriage to Sir William de Willoughby, from near Alford. Thus the dynasty of Willoughby de Eresby was founded, though the fortunes of the estate never recovered from the fire that burnt the house down, after which the family moved to Grimsthorpe permanently. There was supposedly a secret passage from Eresby to Tut Hole, about a mile from Spilsby on the A16.

However, if one seeks the Willoughby family then Spilsby church is the place. Here is a series of monuments of national and even international importance, chronicling the Willoughby and Bertie families. The most amazing memorial is to Richard Bertie and Baroness Willoughby de Eresby, formerly the Duchess of Suffolk, who married one of Henry VIII's closest cronies. A huge wall, it has the dominant figures of a monk and two semi-naked 'wild men', with Bertie and his wife appearing as almost apologetic busts at foot level.

The other monument that attracts visitors is of Catherine Watson, née Willoughby, who died in childbirth in 1610. She is displayed with her baby in a cot at her feet, a haunting sign that tragedy afflicts even the greatest families. The other monuments are preserved in amazingly good condition and show the styles of armour and dress over a long period of English history. It all helps to make Spilsby church a national treasure, yet one which is hardly overrun with tourists.

Another notable feature in the church is a chair made from the timbers of the *Royal George*, a ship which sank at Spithead with the loss of all hands in 1782.

Spilsby as a town owes its growth to the de Bek and Willoughby families. The former founded a market at Spilsby and later a chapel, which is now the parish church; originally it was all in the parish of Eresby.

Spilsby is also famous for Sir John Franklin, one of the extraordinary ranks of Lincolnshire explorers. He was born in 1786 at a house that is now a baker's shop in the Market Place, over a passageway then known as Jennings' Smoot. Franklin joined the Navy in 1800 and had an eventful career; he was once wrecked on a reef off the coast of Australia, was wounded in the battle for New Orleans, and was trapped in the ice during an expedition to find the North Pole in 1818.

From 1825 to 1829 he searched unsuccessfully for the North-West Passage around the top of Canada; despite this failure he was knighted in 1829. In 1845 he began a new attempt to find the route through to the Pacific but was trapped in the ice and lost; he died on 11th June 1847, but this was not known for another twelve years. Various attempts were made to trace what had happened to Franklin and in 1848 an expedition found a cairn left by his men which was said to be 'proof' that he had actually found the Passage. Yet it was to be many years later that the full story of his expedition was uncovered by later explorers.

There is a prominent statue to Franklin in the centre of Spilsby, but less well known is the tablet to him in Spilsby church, erected in 1849.

Spilsby is one of a number of Lincolnshire settlements to

have experienced their own 'great fire'. Spilsby suffered in 1706, when over 100 houses were burnt down in four hours.

The Market Place at Spilsby is separated into two by what was the Town Hall, built in 1764 when Spilsby could claim some importance. Not all visitors were impressed though; when the famous diarist John Byng stayed at the White Hart Inn, he found the mutton 'shockingly large and coarse'. The railways left Spilsby on a very minor branch-line and the Town Hall fell from grace; it was later the Conservative Club and is now a discount shop and petrol station!

Spilsby was also known for a curious 'remedy' against smallpox. It was recommended that the patient (or a relative) should bury a pound of veal in a cellar until it had gone maggoty; then roast the maggots on a wire and put the 'droppings' on the face of the patient. One would have had to be fairly desperate to try that 'medicine'.

Spital in the Street

➤ Lorries and cars thunder through Spital, hardly realising that it is a place that has a name let alone a fascinating history and a unique collection of buildings. It is therefore sad to report that on a recent visit one of the most interesting parts of Spital was in a semi-derelict state and prey to all vandals who cared to stop.

Spital stands right on Ermine Street, a relatively unusual position since there is no other settlement on this road between Lincoln and the M180. The Romans chose a route along the top of the Heath and later villages avoided this due to the lack of reliable water, though I was once told that it was because they were less likely to be attacked by hordes of marauding Vikings. They would get run over if they tried it today.

Because of its position, Spital has always attracted trade from passing travellers and the large house on the east side of the road is an old coaching inn. Some years ago this trade migrated south to Caenby Corner, though even there the hotel is abandoned at the time of writing − only a Little Chef survives. A local link to the glories of the stage-coach is Norton Place, nearby; this was once the home of the Harrisons, who made a fortune from supplying horses for the coaching trade.

But the main reason to stop at Spital lies on the west side of the road. By the time of Edward II there was a hospital here, though this may have had more to do with hospitality for the poor than the treatment of road accident victims. The earliest reference to the hospital is 1204, and it is probable that the settlement took its name from this – Spital, a truncation of 'hospital'. In 1396-9 the hospital was improved by Thomas de Aston, who left lands to provide it with a future income. After the Reformation, though, de Aston's foundation declined and was abandoned, its lands being appropriated by unscruplous local landowners like the Wrays. Early in the 17th century the hospital was revived but it soon ran into problems again and the scandal of de Aston's endowment was discussed in Parliament. The situation was not resolved until 1863, when the endowments were used to pay for the school in Market Rasen that still bears de Aston's name.

The buildings form three sides of a quadrangle, with the road the fourth side. Standing there, the barn-like building to the

The old chapel and almshouses

right is in fact the Sessions House of 1619 which has spent much of its life as a barn! Its intended function reminds us that, though a remote spot, Spital was accessible to many Lindsey folk; The Sessions House was built using some of the materials from the old almshouses, as were the row of cottages in the centre. An old inscription on the Sessions House, 'Fiat Justicia', is almost illegible now.

On the right is the chapel, which may also have reused some of the original materials. Over its door is the inscription, 'I was in 1398; I was not in 1594; I am in 1616'. This refers to the intermittent use of the site for its intended purpose. The chapel was at one time fitted up with the pews and reredos from the Bishop of Lincoln's private chapel at Riseholme, though much of this has gone and the chapel is in a sadly derelict state.

Just to the south-east of Caenby Corner can be seen the remains of an Anglo-Saxon burial mound, said to be the burial place of a prince. Once 8 feet high and nearly 400 feet in circumference, this was excavated in 1850 and found to contain a human skeleton in a seated position. The remains of a horse were also found.

Springthorpe

Springthorpe has an ancient church but its greatest point of interest is a curiosity from more recent history. Preserved inside is a 'Maiden's Garland', surrounding which is a sad tale. Mary Hill was a young bell-ringer who was killed in 1814 when she failed to let the rope run through her fingers. It became entangled round her arm and she was pulled up to the ceiling. She then lost her grasp of the rope and fell to the floor, dashing her head against a stone. After this tragedy the stone was removed and used as the base of the font. At her funeral three white crowns of lilies and white gloves were carried in procession, and it is one of these crowns that is preserved poignantly in the church. Another curiosity is that the west door of the tower has been blocked up with the Anglo-Saxon belfry window.

Off the lane leading to Magin Moor was a spot known as

'Dragon Field'. In this field was a hollow, said to be big enough to hide a combine harvester, and caused by a dragon landing there. The legend records that three dragons had left Wickenby and were flying westwards when one decided to make a landing at Springthorpe, though there seems to be no counter-balancing legend of dragons at Wickenby!

Stainfield (Lindsey)

➤ A remote hamlet on the low-lying clay vale to the east of the Barlings Eau, Stainfield has a long and full history.

Henry de Percy chose this remote place for the site of a priory of Benedictine nuns, which he founded in about 1154 – the remoteness meant that land was more likely to be available and that there would be fewer temptations. However, there are persistent legends that there was a tunnel from Stainfield Priory to Barlings Abbey, so that the monks and nuns could meet fraternally. It has also been suggested that Stainfield Beck was canalised for the same purpose!

After the Dissolution, the estate passed to the Tyrwhitt family. They are said to have got their name from the cry of a lapwing, which betrayed one of their number when he was resting in long grass after fighting a battle to control a bridge. A Tyrwhitt is also said to have killed the 'wild man' of Stainfield Woods, who roamed around stark naked with a large club, which he used to kill several people. Some versions of this tale maintain that it was the wild man who was betrayed by the sound of a startled lapwing, and Tyrwhitt was rewarded with the lands when he subsequently slew him.

The Tyrwhitts built a new mansion on their property, but this was mostly demolished in the 1700s and the destruction completed by fire in 1855. The current house is therefore mid-Victorian, but the earthworks of the priory and the deserted village can be seen. A lonely gate post also survives from earlier building and can be found near the church, which is itself an oddity as it ignores conventional orientation. In the church are various remains of the Tyrwhitts, including a crest showing the wild man and some old funeral clothes – often alluded to as having belonged to the wild man himself.

The wild man of Stainfield

Stamford

➤ One of the finest towns of England, and wholly beyond the scope of this book, Stamford is especially possessed of two things – fine buildings and fine legends. These start with the claim that it was founded in 863 BC by King Bladud, thus predating Rome, and that it once had a university that the Pope closed down.

Perhaps there is an element of truth in that university story . . . In about 1300 some Oxford men did move to Stamford, but were forced to return. They left behind the brass door-knocker on the Brazenose Gate of what was the Greyfriars School and this remained there until 1890, when it too was sent back to Oxford and replaced by a copy.

Daniel Lambert, Britain's fattest man, is buried in St Martin's churchyard. For a while he was keeper of Leicester Prison but his great size – he weighed 52 stones – had commercial potential and he often visited Stamford. A portrait of him was hung up at the George Hotel, where he stayed on many occasions. He used to challenge people to a race, stipulating only that he chose the course, and then walked along the hotel corridor with his rival unable to squeeze past. He died at the Waggon and Horses Inn in 1809.

The Steepings

➤ Great and Little Steeping are hamlets either side of the Steeping river, on low ground prone to flooding. In October 1571 a storm swept most of the Steepings away; a waggon load of willow was caught in the swirling flood, with its body being swept one way and the wheels another.

A mile north is what remains of **Monksthorpe**. There is an early and interesting Baptist chapel of 1701, but more unusual still is the outside pool for baptism by immersion. This is unique in Lincolnshire, and apparently one of only two in the whole country.

The origins of this lonely chapel lie in the Act of Parliament of 1664, when Nonconformists were banned from holding their services within five miles of an Anglican church. Local Baptists therefore chose to meet in a lonely spot where a building could be adapted to their purposes. A boy climbed up a tree to watch for any approaching authorities, and he could get from the tree through a trapdoor in the gable to the main building, thus being able to warn the worshippers.

Between Monksthorpe and Great Steeping is the site of Spilsby airfield, though it was several miles from that town. The construction of the airfield forced the closure of several minor roads, and although they are now open again they have that characteristic 'airfield' look about them.

Stow

➤ Stow is an essential place to visit because of its magnificent and historic church – an extraordinary building for such a small place to boast of.

The word 'stow' is usually taken to mean a holy place, and this certainly seems true here. According to legend, in the seventh century the virginal (though twice married) Saint Etheldreda stopped on the way from Northumbria to Ely and planted her ash staff in the ground: it sprang branches to protect her and a church was built to commemorate the event. This church may have been destroyed by the Danes in about AD 870.

We are more safely in the realm of fact with Bishop Aelfnoth, who built a church at Stow as his 'minster' in about AD 975. This church was later burnt down – perhaps by the Danes again – and replaced in 1034-1050 with a new one under the orders of Bishop Eadnoth. Remigius, the famous Bishop of Lincoln, extended the church in early Norman times. On one of the piers of the chancel can be found a rough drawing of a ship; this is probably meant to be Viking and may be the earliest drawing of a ship known in England. It is a telling reminder of how savage was the threat of the heathen invader.

By tradition Eadnoth founded an abbey at Stow, to which Lady Godiva, wife of Earl Leofric, added a nunnery. However the monks were soon moved away by force and Stow Park became a home for the Bishop of Lincoln.

Tathwell

An interesting village sited at springs on the eastern flank of the Wolds. Just to the south-east are the tumuli of Bully Hill. These were once dug up by treasure seekers who found, so it is said, a heavy iron box buried deep within. They tried to pull it out, but without success, so horses were brought up to help. Eventually all the horses from Tathwell and two other settlements were used. The box slowly moved to the surface but, just as it came into the light, one of the men swore and with a crash it fell back into the pit, the earth collapsed on top of it, and the iron box was never recovered.

This area was dominated by the Chaplin family, one of whom paid for the church at tiny **Haugham** to the south.

Tattershall and Coningsby

These two small towns are now almost a continuous whole, somehow symbolised by the presence of the school and library halfway between them.

The most important of the two settlements historically is Tattershall. This was a significant market town and the central group of buildings around the Market Place still has that character. Worth noting here is the very typical coaching inn, with a carved head over the stable yard that bears a similar character to the villain's head in Horncastle; could there be any connection? The large house on the opposite side has a curiosity on its roof – a miniature 'house' called 'Tom Thumb's House', which is a 15th century roof louvre. It has been suggested that there is a connection between this and the stone slab engraved 'T.Thumb' by the font in Tattershall church. Well, maybe . . .

The history of Tattershall is dominated by Ralph Cromwell, who became Treasurer of England in 1433 and amassed the wealth and lifestyle to suit his status. It was he who rebuilt the castle from about 1434, founded a college and left money for the building of a new church which started in 1469. Near the Market Place is the 'Old College', which was also thought to have been the old church. The new college has also disappeared; it was at the north-east of the church and featured choristers and an organist, as well as staff which included a washerwoman and a swan-keeper. Its main purpose, one suspects, was to pray for Cromwell's soul.

The castle, a famous National Trust property, hardly comes within the scope of this book, but visitors to it should certainly also give some attention to Cromwell's fine church and the slightly older row of almshouses (the Bedehouses) nearby, which were founded in 1440. Originally they were to house 13 poor of both sexes, but were later combined to make 10 units. For a while they were known as 'Gallery Row', supposedly as they housed the 'gallery' singers for the church, though this tale may be untrue. Some of the occupants of the almshouses have clearly kept a profitable eye on the tourist trade in the past, for in 1911 the rules were changed to ban any occupant from 'letting' their conveniences out!

Coningsby church is unusual in the large arch beneath its tower. This is said to have been used by the monks going to Kirkstead, but one suspects this is a rather unlikely explanation, though it may have had a role in other forms of ecclesiastical ritual. On one of the north arches of the church is a carved head of a woman wearing a scold's bridle. Apparently there used to be a real bridle preserved in the vestry. The other striking thing about the church is its large, one-handed clock, said to date from the mid-1600s. Inside the church is also a Dutch flag, used to cover the bodies of three English airmen in the Second World War.

Coningsby is now famous for its RAF base and the attached 'Battle of Britain memorial flight', which preserves and operates a selection of World War II aircraft. The airfield was opened in 1940 and used by 617 Squadron for the raids on Dortmund and Ems, in which they lost five out of every eight Lancasters in one raid.

Just outside the village is the Lea Gate Inn, the start of the lonely road to New York (Lincolnshire!), not far from which is the prosaically named 'No Man's Friend Farm'. The inn always kept a lit lantern outside at night to help travellers across Wildmore Fen, and the bracket can still be seen.

A sad sight in Tattershall is the decaying and derelict old village school, designed by the well-known Victorian architect William Butterfield, and abandoned after a restaurant business failed. It can be contrasted to the well-preserved and attractive old station, near to the river, which provides an excellent base for an art gallery businees. Thus the built heritage of Lincolnshire stands or falls by an accident of economics.

Tealby

Known as one of the prettiest villages in the county, Tealby has little left of its greatest treasure – Bayons Manor. This was a monstrous Victorian Gothic fantasy, part of the medievalist inspiration of Charles Tennyson d'Eyncourt who built it in 1836-42. Its destruction in 1965 was one of the greatest losses of Lincolnshire heritage ever and would now, presumably, have been the cause of regret for its owners. A fantasy such as Bayons Manor would undoubtedly have had commercial possibilities today. Instead all we have are a few pieces, including fragments of the gates which can be seen along Caistor High Street.

Though d'Eyncourt was dismissed by the 'old' families of the county for his pretensions, he designed a house for himself that, in its period, was remarkable and that far exceeds the contemporary Harlaxton.

To the north of Tealby near the Viking Way is Castle Farm, a small-scale Gothic fantasy of a shoebox with battlements. In the village itself is the King's Head Inn, a thatched building of the local building type, 'mud and stud'.

Temple Bruer

Set amidst farm buildings off a lonely country lane, the romantic ruin of Temple Bruer can easily be missed, yet it is one of the most interesting historical remains in Kesteven. Its unusual name reflects the fact that the area became an estate of the Knights Templar in about 1150, when the land was wild heath – the meaning of the 'bruer' part of the name.

The Templars built up a large estate of about 4,000 acres, which they mostly used for sheep farming though enough peasants were persuaded to settle in the area to justify a market. The knights built their usual round church on the site, though the only substantial building that now remains is the south-east tower of the preceptory. Another part of the original building is included in the farmhouse. The Knights Templar at Temple Bruer were arrested in 1308 and imprisoned in Lincoln, their order as a whole being suppressed in 1312 as part of a Europe-wide backlash. The Knights Hospitaller took over the site until it was sold off by Henry VIII, who dined there in 1541.

There is a special car park for visitors to the tower, but it is also a good idea to walk along the green lane that runs from about 3/4 mile east of Temple Bruer up to Temple High Grange. The lane passes the abandoned Warren Houses, the name reflecting the past activity of rabbit farming on the Heath. At Temple High Grange is one of the loneliest churches in Lincolnshire, and attached to it is what was perhaps the loneliest school. Both reflect the fact that population in the area has declined since the 1800s. Returning to the A15, pause to look at Thompson's Bottom farmhouse – probably the loveliest building between Lincoln and Sleaford. Close to it is a visitors' centre, providing further details of this fascinating area.

Tetford

There is a tradition that Tetford was once the scene of a mighty battle in which the Saxon Horsa was defeated by the Britons under Raengieres. Perhaps this theory has been encouraged by ancient earthworks on nearby summits like Hoe Hill.

More welcome visitors to Tetford have included Dr Johnson, who is reported to have played skittles at the White Hart in between his various writings. 'Thrasher' Richardson, the preacher, also spent a lot of time here and threshed corn for six months of the year at Tetford – hence his nickname. There is a tablet commemorating him at the Wesleyan church.

An old Tetford story concerns a woman with magical powers who lived near the church. She was able to change into a hare and at night ran out via the cat flap in her door! Also interested in nocturnal activity was her son, a poacher named Jack. One night he shot at a hare while out in the fields but it got away; as you might guess, when he got home he found his mother in considerable pain but refusing to say what the trouble was. He had to consult the Horncastle 'wise man' before he uncovered the truth.

In 1831 two Tetford men were killed by lightning, and they were buried together in one grave in the churchyard.

Tetney

➤ Tetney used to be a typical marsh-edge village, remote from almost everything except sea breezes and birdsong, but it is now close enough to Grimsby to be affected by the spread of commuting. Without doubt, though, the most interesting thing to see in Tetney is just outside it – the mysterious 'blow wells'.

These are completely natural springs of fresh water to which many legends and stories have somehow become attached. Back in 1901, when the story of Tetney was written by a local clergyman, it was reported that the wells were 'extremely deep and dangerous'. They were so deep in fact that some locals insisted that they 'run through to the Antipodes'. Relying on more trustworthy evidence, the clergyman was also able to report that the wells never froze. The blow wells have provided useful fertiliser to the local imagination, most of the resulting stories consisting of what has fallen into them and never been seen again. There is a legend that one of the ponds got the name of Madame's Blow Well after an important lady; her coach and four horses were swallowed by it. On another occasion a passer-by saw a man's hat floating on the water, and was soon able to rescue its owner from a watery death. 'My horse and gig are down below', the unfortunate traveller was said to have lamented. Common local wisdom was that

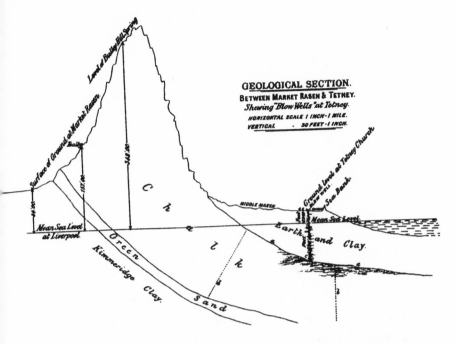

GEOLOGICAL SECTION.
BETWEEN MARKET RASEN & TETNEY.
Shewing "Blow Wells" at Tetney.
HORIZONTAL SCALE 1 INCH - 1 MILE.
VERTICAL · 30 FEET - 1 INCH.

three of the wells were bottomless – and the fourth rather deeper. It was 'well known' that a local farmer had let weights down into the water and found no bottom at all!

There were also delightful stories about a nearby house with a 'young blow well' in its cellar. Apparently, this 'flowed with the tide and oftentimes the owner could not get at his beer or wine when the weather was unusually violent.'

This last story reflects a persistent tradition that the blow wells are affected by the sea. In fact they are springs of water rising from the chalk, which is about 60 feet below the surface. This is the band of chalk that forms the Lincolnshire Wolds further to the west, where the water table is at a height of 300 feet so that the water at Tetney is under considerable pressure. Heavy rain in the Wolds causes the pressure to rise in the wells about three months later, but it actually takes nearly three years for water that has fallen as rain on the Wolds to reach the surface again at Tetney.

Sadly the stories about the wells being 'bottomless' are without foundation. A local sub-aqua club explored them in

1961 and found they only went down about 16 feet – nor did they find the remains of any coach or horses!

Unfortunately blow wells are a declining feature of the Lincolnshire lanscape. Wells at Little Coates were used by Grimsby waterworks from 1863, and were pumped out within about 40 years. Similarly, blow wells at Thornton Abbey suffered from extraction nearby and wells at Laceby were 'lost' by the 1970s.

The area of Tetney is now a nature reserve, to which there is limited public access off the lane to the east of the parish church.

Thorganby

In a valley in the Wolds, Thorganby Hall dates from 1648 and once belonged to the Willoughby family. It has also been a Yarborough property and latterly belonged to the Nainbys.

Peaceful and secluded today, it witnessed exciting events in the Civil War. The house then belonged to William Caldwell, who was a Royalist. In 1643 the house was attacked by a group of Parliamentarians who forced their way in, killed a male servant, and captured Caldwell. He was taken to Lincoln Castle and put into the 'Witch's Hole' – an unpleasantly confined dungeon which he had to bribe his way out of. Mrs Caldwell was also taken to Lincoln and thrown out of the castle gate barely dressed; she was rescued by an apothecary named Strutt, who had his house plundered as a result. Both Caldwell and his wife suffered bad treatment and never really recovered – she died within five months of the attack, and he a few years later.

The rebuilding of the hall in 1648 is taken as evidence that it had suffered much damage during the assault.

A mile to the south is **Swinhope**, the village of the Alington family whose house dates from 1785. One past lady resident at the house was unable to attend the church services but did not like to miss them, so she arranged for an early telephone link to be installed between the lectern and her own quarters at the house so she could take part in comfort. In the parish are two Neolithic burial mounds – Cromwell's Grave (which certainly is not!) on the Binbrook road and Ash Hill near the RAF camp.

Croxby, a mile west of Thorganby, is the very smallest of settlements and possesses one of the tiniest churches in Lincolnshire.

Thornton Abbey

A lonely railway station signifies that Thornton Abbey was once a popular resort for the working people of Grimsby, for whom it made an idyllic spot to picnic at weekends. Now they come from afar, but relatively few tourists make it to one of Lincolnshire's best monastic ruins.

It is most remarkable for the enormous, fortified gatehouse, that dates mostly from the 1380s. This was additionally fortified by a barbican on the outside, remains of which are clearly to be seen. The impressive gateway is decorated with carved figures of religious significance, but nonetheless one feels that this is a castle rather than a monastery. The gatehouse also provided rather comfortable living accommodation, presumably for the abbot.

Once through the gatehouse the visitor walks across a sheep field to the monastic buildings. The ruins are substantial by Lincolnshire standards – most of the other great abbeys of the county having been totally plundered for their building stone.

Henry VIII stayed at the 'College' of Thornton in 1541, but, soon after, it was sold off. Parts of it were pulled down and during this the remains of a monk were found. He had clearly been 'walled up' for some unknown offence, and was supposed to have been sitting at a table with pen and paper. The theory was that he was an abbot, Walter Multon, who had disgraced himself. Another possibility, from the same year, was Thomas Greetham, an abbot who was deposed for no known reason. Perhaps we will never know – the relevant page of the Thornton chronicle has disappeared mysteriously.

The whole site was bought in 1610 by Sir Vincent Skinner, who used some of the stone to build himself a new mansion.

As soon as he had finished, the house fell down for no apparent reason. So was there a curse on Thornton? Well, the stone was also supposed to have been used in the building of Ferriby sluice and that caused endless trouble!

Threekingham

➤ A delightful village with plenty of open spaces not yet built over, and bypassed by the main road.

The name of the village is mythically connected to a great battle between the inevitable Danes and the Saxons, believed to have occurred here in AD 869. Supposedly, three kings were killed and they were buried west of the church, in one of the number of mounds or tumuli that once existed in the area. The most you will see of the three kings today is on the sign of the village pub, where they seem surprisingly cheerful given what may have happened to them here!

The village was important enough to have a charter for a market in 1329, but there is little such commerce today. East of the church are the Laundon stables, one of the entrances to which is marked by an impressive whalebone arch – well worth seeing.

In 1737 Dick Turpin was supposed to have been 'operating' in the district and once called in to a shop in Threekingham to make some purchases. He put a large quantity of oats and two pounds of tea into a long, narrow bag and hid it in Scredington Gorse. He then persuaded a Donington shopkeeper to come and inspect his 'smuggled tea', which the foolish man bought for £11 – not having checked to the bottom of the bag.

In 1787 John Cragg from this village and an 'heiress', Ann Warren of Aslackby, eloped together to Gretna Green.

Thurlby (by Bourne)

The most interesting part of this village is to the east of the main road, near to the church. Here the Roman canal known as Car Dyke is clearly discernible running north to south and closely parallels the route of a Roman road. It was once believed that the moated farm to the north of the church was an abbey.

Elsea Wood, between Thurlby and Bourne, is said to be haunted by the ghost of Nanny Rutt. She was murdered by her lover and thrown into a pool, now called Nanny Rutt's Well.

Torksey

Torksey is one of the most ancient settlements in Lincolnshire, made important by its proximity to the junction of the river Trent and Roman Fosse Dyke canal. Modern Torksey occupies only a fragment of the original site. Its position on the Trent attracted unwelcome visitors, including the Danes. It has also been claimed that at Torksey the missionary Paulinus baptised twelve Christian Saxons, watched by King Edwin of Northumbria.

Torksey retained its religious interest for some centuries, having had a priory and a nunnery. An effigy of Margaret de Moulton, prioress, survived in the churchyard.

Torksey would be worth visiting (if it were open!) for the remains of its 'castle' – really the Elizabethan house of Sir Robert Jermyn and built rather too close to the Trent. In 1645 there was fighting here as Royalists and Parliamentary forces battled for control of the castle.

Tupholme

The lonely remains of Tupholme Abbey can be found on the B1190 west of Bardney, one of a number of monastic ruins along the lower Witham. It was founded in 1190 by Alan and

Gilbert De Nevill, becoming the home for a small community of Premonstratensians.

This remote foundation clearly offered the opportunity for illegal activities. In the 13th century the prior got into trouble for refusing to pay rents to the Crown but matters got worse when a later prior was accused of making forged coins in order to buy corn and wine. The monks also became involved in the illegal horn trade, which they could easily send down the nearby river. The refuse (or 'pith') was buried on the premises. The monks also got into trouble for having a knife fight with their 'rivals' from Revesby, and also for selling wine as French when in fact it came from their own vineyard.

The few remains include part of the refectory and a recessed pulpit, from which a monk read while the others ate. Built on to this is a ruined house which is said to be haunted by a headless woman. On another occasion it was said that a man who lived there was beating his wife when 'Old Nick' appeared, scaring him so much that he never did it again.

Tupholme achieved more recent fame as the scene of a major pop festival in 1972, when thousands of hippies and music fans camped all around – some flying an Australian flag from the old monastic ruins.

Utterby and North Ormsby

➤ Utterby is a small village on the dip slope of the Wolds, North Ormsby a hamlet barely a mile to the west and more fully enfolded by the rising ground.

Utterby is known for its Holy Well, which can be found at Holywell Lane. This was once famous for its miraculous powers, and the superstitious festooned it with rags tied to bushes in honour of the spirits of the place. A little to the west, near the church, is an old packhorse bridge which probably dates from about the 14th century; the bridge is most likely to have been part of a Salt Way from the coast.

North Ormsby was the site of a Gilbertine monastery of the 12th century. The site of it and the deserted medieval village can be clearly seen to the south of the minor road along the valley. Just south of the abbey farm is the famous 'White Lady', a Roman statue placed there in about 1850. Somehow she adds something slightly magical to what is, in any case, a particularly interesting valley.

Waddingham

➤ A feature to look out for in this village is the house on the Market Rasen road which has a clock on its roadside face. The most common explanation of this unusual feature is that the building was put up with the intention of making it the 'Clock Inn', but it was never used for this function.

The parish extends over the Carrs to Brandy Wharf on the river Ancholme, a name reeking of past smuggling activities. The parish church is called St Mary and St Peter, the explanation being that Waddingham used to have two churches but St Peter's disappeared.

Wainfleet

➤ There are two Wainfleets: All Saints, St Mary and the daughter' hamlets of Tofts, Bank and even Clough. The reason for their development was the Steeping river and its use for coastal shipping as a port. This growth was helped by the position of Wainfleet at the north-east end of a low bank, attracting a row of settlements stretching from here to Boston in the middle of an otherwise fenland area.

In fact the story is even more complex than that, for the churchyard of **Wainfleet All Saints** is well to the west of what is now the main settlement, and this is what marks the original site of the town. The reason for the move was the need to seek economic advantage at a time when each of the Wainfleets produced revenues for different monasteries – All Saints belonged to Bardney, while there was also a St Thomas that belonged to Kyme Priory.

So we are left with an oddly disjointed place. All Saints church was only built in 1820, the earlier church to the east having been abandoned. **Wainfleet St Mary** has also abandoned its church, though that survives as a lonely but intact building well to the west, where the original settlement lay. It can still be discerned. Just beyond the modern village of St Mary is **Wainfleet Tofts**, a centre for the medieval salt industry, which has left impressive mounds just north of the A52.

The chief sight of Wainfleet is the remarkable old school building, which was founded in 1484 by the Bishop of Winchester, William Waynflete, a native of the town. Waynflete also founded Magdalen College at Oxford, and had a spell as Lord Chancellor. His school was designed largely to match the similar institution at Tattershall.

The other remarkable sight in Wainfleet is Barkham Street. It is as if the visitor has suddenly been transported from a quiet Lincolnshire market town to the industrial terraces of an overcrowded Victorian London. The street bears no relation to the design or layout of any of the rest of the town, for it was built on land given to the Bethlehem hospital ('Bedlam') of London by Sir Edward Barkham, and the houses were designed by London architect Sydney Smirke without any thought of Lincolnshire conditions. The whole street has the appearance of being transported from south London.

Wainfleet is famous in Lincolnshire today for Bateman's Brewery, the only brewery in the county and of which it is justly proud. The brewery's emblem features the old mill at the brewery site. The brewery is usually described as the Salem Brewery, taking its name from the bridge close by; this word may be a corruption of Sailholme, once a small island to the south of the bridge. It had a monastic chapel from about 1165 but by the 1350s was in a state of ruin, though it was revived after a series of miracles were attributed to the spot! Alan Wastelere dreamt that St Edmund told him to repair the ruined chapel in about 1376, following which all manner of good things happened to him. The chapel has now gone again, but perhaps someone might be tempted to see if St Edmund's powers still work . . .

Walesby

➤ Walesby is well known due to its position on the Viking Way in the heart of the Wolds, and especially because the old village church – which is over 300 ft above sea level – has been adopted as the 'Ramblers' Church'.

It seems likely that the first church was built in this inconvenient position as it used a pagan site (there were Anglo-Saxon burials here), but the village grew lower down the hill where there was a water supply. In 1881 an iron church was built in the village and by the 1920s the original church was in a sorry state of decay. It was restored in 1931 and became the 'Ramblers' Church' from 1932. As such it is preserved in an interesting state and anything but the antiseptic museum that such places can become.

Half a mile east of the church was an important Roman villa covering an area of about 300 square yards. Near here was discovered, in 1959, the 'Walesby tank' which is believed to have been a baptismal font for Roman Christians.

North from Walesby is **Normanby-le-Wold**, Lincolnshire's highest settlement and traditionally pronounced 'Norramby'. The hill from here down to Claxby is said to be haunted by the ghost of a headless woman. No doubt the number of tumuli in the area help to stir the local imagination, for there are also stories of 'shag boys' who haunt the Bluestone Heath road. Ghostly hoofbeats have also been heard cantering alongside and then disappearing.

Just west of Normanby is **Claxby**, another small village. There is an old ice-house near the church, used to store winter's ice into the spring and summer. On the chancel arches are some very strange faces, rather like the effects of a child trying to contort its face to annoy a parent!

Well

➤ The hilltop church at Well and the view from there over the house, lake and valley must be one of the most satisfying vistas in Lincolnshire and is well worth a visit. The whole landscape is dominated by the fashions of the early 18th century, and the church was rebuilt in this position to add punctuation to the view from Well Hall. The interior of the church is also a wonderful survival in itself with well-preserved 18th century furnishings, though the house is now used as a private school.

In the tiny churchyard is one grave of special note: William Dudley, a gamekeeper, was murdered by a poacher in 1839.

Welton-le-Marsh

➤ A small marsh-edge village with some interesting details. In the woods to the north is Thwaite Hall, standing on a site that is at least medieval and was clearly well defended. The village that was once here has gone. There used to be a Thwaite Fair every Lady Day, but the place is better known now for the odd building of chalk attached to the main house. It has been said that this was a small Augustinian chapel and even a 'punishment cell' for bad monks from Bardney, or more probably a cell of Thornton Abbey.

Less than half a mile east, at **Hanby**, is Castle Hill. There was said to be a secret underground passage between here and Thwaite, but there was never a proper castle here, though a pre-Roman fortification has been suggested.

Welton's church fell down in 1791 and was replaced with a new one. In 1914 the font of the old church was discovered in use as a cattle trough near the church — hence the church now has two fonts.

West Halton

➤ North of the church, in the recreation field, is a large mound. Over the years this has been identified successively as the tomb of a Roman soldier, the tomb of a Saxon warrior and a mound on which a mill once stood. One suspects that the fact that it now supports a slide suggests someone favours the latter explanation!

Half a mile to the south is the hamlet of **Coleby**. When the old hall here was being repaired, a skeleton was found hidden inside. A large sum of money has also been found hidden in a chimney!

Willingham by Stow

➤ In days gone by the tradition in Willingham church was for men to sit on the left and women on the right. This was meant to preserve decorum, so no doubt the villagers at Willingham would have been shocked to hear that at **Corringham** women went to sit with the men, 'the reins of their modesty being relaxed'. Mind you, that was in 1311!

Between the village and Sandebus Farm was once a low-lying area of bog. Traditionally it was believed that a man and his horse had once been swallowed up in the bog, which was said to be inhabited by snakes ten feet long. It has now been drained.

The lane from Willingham to Sandebus Farm bends sharply, at which point a bridleway runs south and there was a track leading to Normanby, thus making a sort of crossroads. Here a gypsy woman was once buried, having apparently died in childbirth.

To the east is Turpin Farm, one of the many places in the area associated with Dick Turpin who was said to prey on travellers along Ermine Street. To the south-east is the hamlet of **Coates**, in the middle of which is a beautifully preserved little church with an astonishing interior – one of the few places where you can still get a close look at the rood screen. Seemingly even the Reformation forgot about such an isolated hamlet.

Willoughby

This village is connected with the heritage of Lincolnshire by the link between its name and the great Willoughby family, though it was largely an accident of marriage that allowed the minor gentry of Willoughby to connect themselves with the de Bec family of Eresby.

The village is at the centre of several prehistoric features, the closest of which is the Butterbump, a series of tumuli about a mile east on the lane to Cumberworth. A mile west, near **Claxby-by-Alford**, is another group of long barrows known as Deadmen's Graves.

Willoughby was a marshland parish, with the main village situated at the edge of the solid ground but its lands extending into the marsh proper. Parts of this were later colonised by its people – **Sloothby** and **Bonthorpe** were thus served by Willoughby church. Sloothby gained a chapel of its own in medieval times but this had clearly gone by the Victorian era, when a chancel was added to a pre-existing school building to create a hybrid school/church in 1880.

Willoughby is also well known as the birthplace of Captain John Smith in 1579. A soldier and adventurer who was once enslaved by the Turks, he sailed to America in 1607 where he was captured by Indians; he escaped only by the help of Pocahontas, the chief's daughter. After many other adventures he became one of the founding fathers of Virginia and helped to develop the colony of Maine. A window in the church commemorates Smith.

Claxby-by-Alford is a tiny hamlet close to Willoughby. The village itself was largely south-east of the hall, but has been planted over with trees. The hall itself has had a varied existence, having been swapped for Well rectory in 1836 so that it became a rectory and the squire moved to Well. Perhaps this is a comment on how well clergy lived in those days. The area is also known for its supposed tunnels, at least three have been referred to though they seem to be connected with chalk workings rather than anything more romantic.

Winceby

➤ Winceby lies on the rolling Lincolnshire Wolds east of Horncastle and is famous for its Civil War battle of 1643. Parliamentary forces under the Earl of Manchester had advanced from Boston on 9th October and began a siege of the Royalist stronghold at Old Bolingbroke. The next day Manchester's cavalry was surprised by some Royalist reinforcements which attacked them at Horncastle and Thimbleby, and they were forced back.

This success encouraged the Royalists to believe they could chase the Parliamentary army back to Boston, but on 11th October they were intercepted by Parliamentary cavalry at Winceby and utterly routed. It was an important victory as it opened up east Lincolnshire to the control of Parliament, and Lincoln itelf surrendered on 20th October.

The Ordnance Survey shows the battlefield as being close to the junctions of the A158 and A1115 roads, but in fact it was at the junction of the A1115 and the more modern road to Old Bolingbroke via Asgarby. Royalist forces were pushed back along the Horncastle road and were trapped by hedges and a gate at a valley called Slash Hollow, close to a bend in the A1115. A colourful legend claims that this valley ran ankle-deep in blood at the time of the battle, which is commemorated by a recent memorial at Winceby House.

Near to this there is another one of Lincolnshire's glacial erratic boulders, also with its own fund of stories. Of course rumours abounded that there was treasure beneath it. One legend relates that some men tied horses to the boulder and when it began to move one of them exclaimed, 'Let God or the Devil come now for we have it', and in a trice the Devil himself was seen standing upon the stone! The stone fell back into its resting place, but the Devil left a claw mark upon it.

When another attempt was made to move the stone a black mouse ran out from under it and scared the horses. Eventually it was buried by digging a hole alongside it. Within about the last 20 years the stone has been moved to the roadside, so visitors should avoid the temptation to dig it up in the search for treasure.

Winceby is worth visiting today for the very attractive Snipe Dales country park. Visitors can either park at the nature reserve end, nearer the village, or further east at the country park itself. Short walks to suit all tastes can be made and the landscape varies remarkably within a small area.

Winteringham and Winterton

━ These two substantial settlements are the last ones on the limestone edge before it reaches the Humber. This part of the county, known to the Romans as Ermine Street, met the Humber here, and there was a ferry enabling travellers to reach York – though this route was later replaced for most traffic by the more westerly way by Till Bridge Lane. Nonetheless the site of a Roman settlement can be seen beside the A1077 south-east of Winteringham, though the most prominent feature there now is the chalybeate spring. Perhaps this is the spring, or possibly the one near Gate End Farm, where until about 1800 an iron ladle was kept for the convenience of travellers; close to this the farmhouse at Eastfield is inscribed 'Pray play and sing God save the King 1796'. A substantial number of Roman remains have been found in the district, including the remains of timber jetty in the Humber when the water is very low.

The edge of the Humber here is by no means a stable feature. There is evidence that the Humber was once much broader and more shallow than it is now. In the late 1700s the people of Winteringham were concerned about land being lost to the Humber and conceived a plan to fill a French warship with chalk rubble, then to sink it so that it would act as a breakwater. However, they scuppered their own plan by removing all the best wood first, so that when the ship sank the chalk simply washed out of it.

A couple of decades ago the theory about the Romans having a ford rather than a ferry across the Humber was put to the test by Lord Noel Buxton, who tried to walk across at low tide. He got most of the way, but was stopped by a deep channel at the Brough side. Saint Etheldreda, the foundress of the abbey at Ely, had no such problems, she was carried across 'by a gentle breeze' when making her epic journey to the Fens.

During the 1700s Winteringham was considered something of a poor town. It was almost surrounded by marsh and was thought of as old-fashioned. Smoking tobacco in the street was banned (there was a fine of two shillings) and the bell of an old chapel was kept on a wooden frame by the pillory, which had 'a ridiculous appearance'.

Winterton is a bigger town, though now eclipsed by Scunthorpe. A man buried in the churchyard there made his own tombstone and cut most of the inscription, then used it as a table until he died, when a friend finished off the inscription. He also made his own coffin, which he used as a cupboard. Buried on the north side of the church in about 1785 was Cawkwell Greeve; he disliked the superstition that the north side was 'the Devil's side' so insisted on being buried there. For many years it was traditional to crumble bread for the birds on his tomb, a custom which now seems to have been a victim of churchyard clearance. Some odd structures at 53 West Street are the work of William Fowler, an antiquarian, who lived there in the 1820s and pursued his own interests by building various follies.

Witham on the Hill

➤ A delightful village in the rolling limestone countryside of south Lincolnshire. The road through the village, though it has some nasty bends, is almost a joy because of the rapidly changing vistas that appear and vanish. A good example of this is the Pillared Cottage, at the eastern approach to the village.

There are several features of interest, starting with Palace Farm which once belonged to the Bishops of Lincoln – hence its name. Behind the farm is an unusual pyramidal dovecote, standing rather alone in the middle of pasture.

Between Palace Farm and the church is the old village school, adorned with a moral slogan: 'Train up a child the way he should go and when he is old he will not part from it'.

Beyond the church the village suddenly opens up into a large

The village stocks

green. Tucked in one corner of this, almost below the level of the road, the alert visitor will find the old village stocks. These are well-preserved and roofed over, hardly in keeping with the original intention of making life uncomfortable for miscreants.

Withern

Once the home of the Fitzwilliam family, who dominated the area between here and the coast at Mablethorpe. Their house was at Castle Hill, a moated area east of the church (no longer in use).

There is also an unusual earthwork at the west end of the village, with banks and ditches, but little is known about it.

A mile to the east is **Strubby**, where 'Hermitage Hill' once yielded some bones, so it is assumed that there was a chapel here to mark a burial ground. Near this point was once an ancient oak, said to have been 1,000 years old and four yards in diameter.

184

A mile to the south-west is the hamlet of **Tothill**, where the church has been demolished. It derives its name from 'Toot Hill', a medieval motte and bailey which never really grew into a castle, and was once surrounded with marshland.

Wold Newton and surrounding hamlets

➤ The eastern dip slope of the Wolds is an area of tiny hamlets, many of which have decayed from medieval times so that they barely exist.

Wold Newton is what passes for a 'large' village in the area, though its growth has always been controlled by the Yarborough estate. Scallows Hall, over a mile to the south and in woodland, is an 18th century hunting lodge built for Lord Grimthorpe.

East and **West Ravendale** are small and very rural. The chief feature of interest here is the remains of the priory at West Ravendale, founded in about 1202. The rather romantic ruin of a small chapel still survives on a hill above Priory Farm. The village of West Ravendale had lost most of its people by the 14th century.

East of Wold Newton there is a succession of 'lost' villages with relatively little remaining. **North Cadeby** had lost its people by the mid 1300s and seeming to have a similar future is Cadeby Hall, a large 18th century house long abandoned. Either side and within less than a mile can be found other 'lost' villages – **Beesby** and **Wyham**.

The house at Cadeby was linked with a number of stories about secret underground passages which were said to start in the hillside to the south-east of the house. One apparently went to Wyham House, where it came up in the schoolroom. Another was linked to a rumour (untrue!) that once there had been monks at Cadeby and they used a tunnel to get to the nuns at North Ormsby. The tunnels were supposedly blocked by chains but these had to be removed after continuous noises at night suggested that someone was not happy about this blockage.

There are a number of pools at Cadeby. One of these, rectangular with a stone surround, was known as the Monk's Bath.

185

Woodhall Spa

➤ Woodhall is, in effect, Lincolnshire's 'premier' resort, for it began to develop in a desultory sort of way before Skegness was really on the map. The original settlement is now the hamlet of **Old Woodhall**, to the north, but Woodhall Spa was started as the accidental result of a scheme to find coal in Lincolnshire.

John Parkinson was a local entrepreneur who, among other schemes, wanted to build a 'city' at New Bolingbroke. In 1811 he began a scheme to sink a shaft in search of coal in the woods at what is now Woodhall Spa. The shaft reached a depth of 1,200 ft but no coal was discovered, so it was abandoned. However water flowed out of the shaft and this was used by Thomas Hotchkin of Woodhall Lodge, who must have been very pleased when a lady from Horsington declared that it had cured her rheumatism.

Hotchkin saw a business opportunity where Parkinson had failed. The water was declared to be good for skin diseases too, and so in 1838 Hotchkin built a pump room and baths, with a hotel following the next year. The growth of the town was encouraged by the formation of a development syndicate in 1886.

In 1905 Grace Maple, the wealthy daughter of the furniture tycoon, chose to settle in Woodhall Spa. What is now the Petwood Hotel began life as her home. Miss Maple was first married to Baron von Eckardstein, then in 1910 she married Captain Weigall, the land agent of Blankney. Their house was used to treat wounded soldiers during the First World War, but is especially famous because of its connection with events of the Second World War.

During World War II Woodhall Spa became renowned for its connection with 617 Squadron – the Dambusters. The remains of the airfield can be easily seen to the north of the road to Tattershall. The Petwood Hotel was converted into the officers' mess, but not without some unforeseen consequences. When planning for a hazardous mission over enemy territory, the RAF officers were issued with revolvers which they proceeded to practise with by shooting up various

The Wellington memorial

statues that adorned the Petwood's lawns. 617 Squadron is now commemorated by a fine memorial in the middle of Woodhall Spa. The two most famous officers of 617 Squadron, Guy Gibson and Leonard Cheshire, both spent some time at the Petwood.

Woodhall was also a target for enemy bombers. In August 1942 a parachute mine demolished most of the Royal Hotel in the centre of the town, so that the Mall Tavern is all that remains. The building is an interesting one, especially its rustic doorway.

The spa itself fell into disuse and neglect. In 1983 the buildings over the spa well finally collapsed. However, an interesting building that does survive in the woods is the 'Kinema in the Woods', which began life as a tennis pavilion.

To the north-east of Woodhall Spa, towards Martin Moor, can be found a gaunt ruin known as the 'Tower on the Moor'. This is related to Tattershall Castle both in its architecture and its owner, but its purpose is something of a mystery; it was probably a form of ornate hunting lodge, but seems to have been little used.

Due north of Woodhall Spa lies Thimbleby Moor, where a rather surprising monument can be found beside a quiet country lane. In 1844 Colonel Elmhirst decided to put up a memorial to the Duke of Wellington, 36 ft high and surmounted with a bust of the Iron Duke. Behind the monument is Waterloo Wood, planted with acorns just after the battle.

Sources & Bibliography

Much of this book has depended on personal observation and help from various individuals. I am always grateful for such assistance. Printed sources that have been used include the following:

ANON *A Guide to Tennyson's Lincolnshire* (1973)
ANON *St Mary's Stow in Lindsey* (1992)
BEASTALL, T.W. *Agricultural Revolution in Lincolnshire* (1978)
BENNETT & BENNETT (eds) *Historical Atlas of Lincolnshire* (1993)
BRAKSPEAR, H. *Bardney Abbey* (1922)
CROWDER, T. *History of Bardney Village* (1925)
DUDLEY, H.E. *History & Antiquities of Scunthorpe* (1931)
EKBERG, C. *Book of Cleethorpes* (1986)
EKWALL, E. *Oxford Dictionary of English Place Names* (1960)
HALPENNY, B. *Action Stations* (1981)
HILL, F. *Medieval Lincoln* (1965)
HILL, F. *Tudor & Stuart Lincoln* (1956)
HODGETT, G.A.J. *Tudor Lincolnshire* (1975)
HOLMES, C. *Seventeenth Century Lincolnshire* (1980)
KIGHTLY, C. *Churches of the Western Wolds* (1991)
LAMBERT, M. & WALKER, R. *Boston, Tattershall & Croyland* (1930)
LEACH, T. *Lincolnshire Country Houses and Their Families (various volumes)*
LFWI *Lincolnshire Village Book* (1990)
MAY, J. *Prehistoric Lincoln* (1976)
OWEN, D.M. *Church and Society in Medieval Lincolnshire* (1981)
PEVSNER, HARRIS and ANTRIM *The Buildings of England: Lincolnshire* (1989 edition)
PLATTS, G. *Land and People in Medieval Lincolnshire* (1985)
ROSENTHALL, D. *The Royal Village of Old Bolingbroke* (1988)
RUDDOCK, J.G. *Boothby Graffoe & Somerton Castle* (1974)

RUDKIN, E.H. *Lincolnshire Folklore*
SHAW, G. *Old Grimsby* (1897)
SMITH, M. *Stamford Myths and Legends* (1991)
STREET, B. *Historical Notes on Grantham* (1857)
TROTTER, J.R. *Freiston with Butterwick* (1936)
WRIGHT, N.R. *Lincolnshire Towns & Industry* (1982)

Periodicals: Green's *Lincolnshire Villages* series, *Lincolnshire Life, Past & Present, Lincolnshire Notes & Queries.*

I have also found old OS maps annotated by the County Archaeological Service very useful in locating forgotten gems of Lincolnshire – and in finding that some are no longer there!

Most of the above may be consulted at the Lincoln Local Studies Library, to whose staff I am especially grateful. I would also like to award a special vote of thanks to Hilary Healey who read the final proofs for me at short notice and made a number of useful suggestions.

Index